POINTS of DEPARTURE

7 Challenges to the American Evangelical Church

by Jim Thomson
foreword by Scott Linklater

Points of Departure

7 Challenges to the American Evangelical Church

By Jim Thomson

Published by:
Joshua Tree Publishing

www.JoshuaTreePublishing.com

All rights reserved. No part of this book may be reproduced or transmitted in any form or by any means, electronic or mechanical, including photocopying, recording or by any information storage and retrieval system without written permission from the author, except for the inclusion of brief quotations in a review.

Scriptures from the Bible are used with permission of publishers. Please see Bible Acknowledgements for citations.

Copyright © 2010 Jim Thomson

ISBN: 0-9823703-8-5
13-Digit: 978-0-9823703-8-4

Cover by Expectation Media
www.expectationmedia.com

Thanks to Sandi Frederick, Laurie Klein, Scott Linklater, Dan Smith and Laurie Thomson for their assistance in editing this manuscript.

Printed in the United States of America

For Ben and Molly,
fellow strangers and sojourners
on the earth.

Bible Translation Acknowledgements

Several Bible translations and versions were used in this book to express God's Word. We appreciate the publishers' permissions for using their work.

Unless otherwise indicated, all Scripture quotations are taken from The Holy Bible, English Standard Version, copyright © 2001 by Crossway Bibles, a division of Good News Publishers. Used by permission. All rights reserved.

Scriptures taken from the Holy Bible, New International Version®, NIV®. Copyright © 1973, 1978, 1984 by Biblica, Inc.™ Used by permission of Zondervan. All rights reserved worldwide.

Scripture quotations marked NLT are taken from the Holy Bible, New Living Translation, copyright © 1996, 2004. Used by permission of Tyndale House Publishers, Inc., Wheaton, Illinois 60189. All rights reserved.

Table of Contents

Bible Translation Acknowledgements		4
Foreword		7
Introduction		9
Chapter One	What Is Commendable?	11
Chapter Two	What Is Attractive?	25
Chapter Three	What Is Presentable?	39
Chapter Four	What Is Wealth?	61
Chapter Five	What Is Leadership?	77
Chapter Six	What Is Suffering?	93
Chapter Seven	What Is Strong?	111
Afterword		127
Jim Thomson's Connection		131

Foreword

*"If today's church does not recapture the
sacrificial spirit of the early church, it will lose
its authenticity, forfeit the loyalty of millions,
and be dismissed as an irrelevant social club
with no meaning for the twentieth century."*
–Dr. Martin Luther King

This is true for the twenty-first century as well.

Written from a Birmingham jail in 1963 by Dr. King, these chilling words carry truth that transcends the civil rights movement and speak to us about the current state of church culture.

Our organizations and denominations have become disconnected from the reasons why they started in the first place. We've substituted business models for biblical principles and exchanged spiritual truths for catchy alliterations. The organizations have become more concerned with their own survival than with their founding purposes. This is unacceptable, but it doesn't have to remain this way.

We can reverse this humanistic influence and return to our roots – but it will take hard work, surrender, and deconstruction.

In the same letter by Dr. King, this second truth bounds forth:

> "Human progress never rolls in on wheels of inevitability; it comes through the tireless efforts of men willing to be co-workers with God, and without this hard work, time itself becomes an ally of the forces of social stagnation. We must use time creatively, in the knowledge that the time is always ripe to do right."

Our "work" is to retrace our steps back to the Word of God and let the Bible reshape our thinking and methods—no holds barred, no sacred cows, no tables left unturned. Now is the time. The harvest is ripe.

Pastor and missionary Jim Thomson approaches these topics with an insider's viewpoint and addresses the challenges that face the American evangelical church if it is to remain effective and spiritually relevant.

As you read Points of Departure, allow yourself to be undone and deconstructed, and ask the Holy Spirit to rebuild what remains. You'll find your foundations stronger, your heart focused, and you'll hear the still, small voice remind you that:

"My yoke is easy, and My burden is light."

Scott Linklater

Introduction

I love the Church. It's only right and appropriate that I should, after all, since Jesus commanded us to love each other. However, as much as I love her—should I insert here that some of my best friends are Christians?—I have become increasingly troubled about the condition in which she exists today. I'm concerned about us, first and foremost—regardless of how we tally the numbers of our gatherings—because we're failing in some essentially biblical ways in the value system that undergirds what we do and, strangely, seem to be unaware of it.

I believe the Church is in need of a sweeping transformation. Will this transformation be a revival? Yes, although the changes that are necessary will be the result of that revival, not the cause of it. The Lord is at work today, by His grace, calling Western Christians to a radical faith in Jesus Christ. When these believers hear His call to give up their lives for Him, they begin to become increasingly dissatisfied and frustrated with the institutional church structures because those constructs tend to impede the spiritual growth of these fervent disciples rather than encourage it. Why is that? What is it about the way we "do church" that actually weakens us?

What I advocate in this book is not a new way of doing things, a new step-by-step method. I'm advocating a sincere, paradigm-changing look at the values that are promoted in the Bible. I'm at war with the principles that currently underlie how we have come to function in this organization that we call church. I'm calling for a ship-righting reform of those principles. However, this transformation must flow from an intimate, life-denying love for God. Without that, we're simply—vainly—singing in the square, promoting superficial alterations that will die within a generation.

This radical set of values is ancient—as old as the New Testament—and will be extraordinarily difficult for us to realize. The book you're about to read is challenging, and it should be. We are losing the passion which Jesus requires for a dynamic life with Him, and subsequently, the war for precious human souls.

Chapter One

What Is Commendable?

"While it is well enough to leave footprints on the sands of time, it is even more important to make sure they point in a commendable direction."
~James Branch Cabell

"If I must boast, I will boast of the things that show my weakness."
~Paul, the apostle

Dave Hutchinson*, pastor of a new church plant in the urban core of a nearby city, called and invited me to have a cup of coffee at a downtown Starbucks recently. I admired Dave. He was attempting a very demanding task. As we discussed his struggles, he told me about the difficulty of living in the shadow of the mega-church from which his little work was birthed.

"I spoke at their men's breakfast a couple of months ago, and although I know it's dumb, I really, really wanted one of the men's group leaders to tell Chris (the pastor of the mega-church) what a great job I'd done. I know it's not right. But I really, really wanted that to happen."

As we continued our conversation, Dave related the pressure he felt due to the lack of successful results in his ministry. Yes, he and his people were reaching out to the community, but they weren't growing. "A healthy church is a growing church," he told me. He wondered if that was why he felt that Chris treated him like a youngster, a newbie, and not like an equal, although Dave was forty-five years old. I told him I understood how he felt, and that it takes us awhile to know who we are in the ministry, regardless of what or how anyone else is doing. He agreed that needed to happen.

We talked on the phone a couple of months later. Nothing he was doing seemed to be working. "Regardless of the results," he said, "I just wish they would tell me they were proud of me."

"I'm proud of you, Dave," I responded.

He wept.

These conversations brought up several questions that for months began turning over in my mind: What do we value in the Church? What is commendable? What kind of people are we looking for in our pastors and leaders? Are the criteria we use for making these value judgments biblical?

The answer to this last question is yes—and no.

Yes, certainly, we follow the guidelines that Paul

wrote in his letters to Timothy and Titus. Here are the qualifications he listed for elders or overseers in his letter to Titus:

> He must not be arrogant or quick-tempered or a drunkard or violent or greedy for gain, but hospitable, a lover of good, self-controlled, upright, holy, and disciplined. He must hold firm to the trustworthy word as taught, so that he may be able to give instruction in sound doctrine and also to rebuke those who contradict it
> (Titus 1:7b-9).

To Timothy, Paul said:

> Therefore an overseer must be above reproach, the husband of one wife, sober-minded, self-controlled, respectable, hospitable, able to teach, not a drunkard, not violent but gentle, not quarrelsome, not a lover of money. He must manage his own household well, with all dignity keeping his children submissive, for if someone does not know how to manage his own household, how will he care for God's church? He must not be a recent convert, or he may become puffed up with

conceit and fall into the condemnation of the devil. Moreover, he must be well thought of by outsiders, so that he may not fall into disgrace, into a snare of the devil. Deacons likewise must be dignified, not double-tongued, not addicted to much wine, not greedy for dishonest gain. They must hold the mystery of the faith with a clear conscience. And let them also be tested first; then let them serve as deacons if they prove themselves blameless. Their wives likewise must be dignified, not slanderers, but sober-minded, faithful in all things. Let deacons each be the husband of one wife, managing their children and their own households well (1 Timothy 3:2-12).

Generally speaking, Paul is talking about character and moral issues in these passages. However, the only two things that separate the qualifications required here from those of an "ordinary" believer are maturity and experience—"let them also be tested first"—and an ability to teach. Everything else listed is what we in the Church expect from anyone who would want to follow Jesus Christ. However, there are additional qualifications if we truly want to be a leader like Paul, although we have to search just a little harder to find them.

Let's look at this passage from 2 Corinthians 6:3-10, where Paul is attempting to convince the Corinthian church that he is indeed a leader, worthy of their respect.

> We put no obstacle in anyone's way, so that no fault may be found with our ministry, but as servants of God we commend ourselves in every way: by great endurance, in afflictions, hardships, calamities, beatings, imprisonments, riots, labors, sleepless nights, hunger; by purity, knowledge, patience, kindness, the Holy Spirit, genuine love; by truthful speech, and the power of God; with the weapons of righteousness for the right hand and for the left; through honor and dishonor, through slander and praise. We are treated as impostors, and yet are true; as unknown, and yet well known; as dying, and behold, we live; as punished, and yet not killed; as sorrowful, yet always rejoicing; as poor, yet making many rich; as having nothing, yet possessing everything.

Let's compare how we in the contemporary church in the United States commend ourselves, with how Paul commended himself. Admittedly, all Christians share many of the hardships and attributes that Paul lists here. Many of us exhibit the fruit of lives lived in the Spirit that are included in this passage: knowledge, patience, kindness and genuine love. What is notable, though, is not so much what is present, but what is absent. In order to commend himself, nowhere does Paul bring up how many churches he had planted, and we know that he planted a few. Nor does he reveal how many people he had brought to a saving knowledge of Jesus Christ—and we know he was an evangelist. There is no mention of the number of healings or deliverances—and we know people were healed through his ministry. We don't read here about the numerical size of the meetings Paul led. What we see in Paul's apostolic defense is a catalog of affliction, virtue, sacrifice and loss, as well as fruit of the Spirit.

> *Paul valued sacrifice and character.*
>
> *We value numbers and results.*

There is a difference in what Paul valued in ministry and what we value. Paul valued sacrifice and character.

We value numbers and results.

We see this again in Paul's apostolic defense in 2 Corinthians 11:21b-33:

But whatever anyone else dares to boast of—I am speaking as a fool—I also dare to boast of that. Are they Hebrews? So am I. Are they Israelites? So am I. Are they offspring of Abraham? So am I. Are they servants of Christ? I am a better one—I am talking like a madman—with far greater labors, far more imprisonments, with countless beatings, and often near death. Five times I received at the hands of the Jews the forty lashes less one. Three times I was beaten with rods. Once I was stoned. Three times I was shipwrecked; a night and a day I was adrift at sea; on frequent journeys, in danger from rivers, danger from robbers, danger from my own people, danger from Gentiles, danger in the city, danger in the wilderness, danger at sea, danger from false brothers; in toil and hardship, through many a sleepless night, in hunger and thirst, often without food, in cold and exposure. And, apart from other things, there is the daily pressure on me of my anxiety for all the churches. Who is weak, and I am not weak? Who is made to fall, and I am not indignant? If I must boast, I will boast of the things that show my weakness. The

> God and Father of the Lord Jesus, he who is blessed forever, knows that I am not lying. At Damascus, the governor under King Aretas was guarding the city of Damascus in order to seize me, but I was let down in a basket through a window in the wall and escaped his hands.

There was a myriad of things Paul could have boasted about. But he makes it clear that if he is to do any boasting, it will be about his *weakness.*

I guess he wasn't interested in speaking at conferences.

Imagine if you will, a promotional flyer for a Dynamic Spiritual Life Conference, with Paul as the main speaker:

"This year's conference will be held at the beautiful Boca Raton Opulent Inn. Our keynote speaker will be a man known all over the world: Paul the apostle. He will tell us how to make maximum spiritual impact for Jesus Christ in our world! Learn how to be hungry and poor! Learn what to do when you get beat up by an angry mob! Learn how to be weak and in constant danger! Your ministry will be greatly enriched!"

There isn't any tidy outline in these passages in 2 Corinthians on how to become a leader, a topic we have almost been obsessed with—only a testimony, again, of sacrifice and loss. Once more, no mention from Paul about what we too easily call the "fruit of ministry"—

salvations, baptisms, church plants—no numbers in any way whatsoever. Paul is saying, "Do you want proof that I'm an apostle? Let me tell you about how I've sacrificially offered my life to Jesus."

We don't hear this kind of talk very much, at least in my experience, when we want to know how to become pastors and leaders.

Numbers. We all say they don't matter. Pastors of mega-churches say they don't matter. Pastors of medium-sized churches say they don't matter. Pastors of very small churches say they don't matter. We keep saying it, and perhaps some of us believe it. But let's have a moment of transparency here. Scan quickly and make a list of notable pastors. Why are they notable? For any of the reasons Paul mentions? No. They are notable either because they have a large church or they've written a book. What we consider commendable for leaders and what the Bible considers commendable are at odds with each other.

Let's take a quick look at Hebrews 11:32-38. This portion of Scripture is often the focus of our attention because it is included in this wonderful chapter about faith.

> And what more shall I say? For time would fail me to tell of Gideon, Barak, Samson, Jephthah, of David and Samuel and the prophets—who through faith conquered kingdoms, enforced justice, obtained

promises, stopped the mouths of lions, quenched the power of fire, escaped the edge of the sword, were made strong out of weakness, became mighty in war, put foreign armies to flight. Women received back their dead by resurrection. Some were tortured, refusing to accept release, so that they might rise again to a better life. Others suffered mocking and flogging, and even chains and imprisonment. They were stoned, they were sawn in two, they were killed with the sword. They went about in skins of sheep and goats, destitute, afflicted, mistreated—of whom the world was not worthy—wandering about in deserts and mountains, and in dens and caves of the earth.

After telling us about Abraham, Isaac, Jacob, Joseph, Moses and Rahab, the author of Hebrews lists Gideon, Barak, Samson, Jephthah, David and Samuel, the prophets and others he doesn't name. These are called the heroes of faith.

> *The gist of this amazing chapter isn't the size of the tasks done by men and women but what it cost for them to believe God*

There are tangible accomplishments here. However, those who did achieve something which was quantifiable accomplished it by faith when they were *in extremis*. The gist of this amazing chapter isn't the size of the tasks done by men and women but *what it cost for them* to believe God: "They were stoned, they were sawn in two, they were killed with the sword. They went about in skins of sheep and goats, destitute, afflicted, mistreated—of whom the world was not worthy—wandering about in deserts and mountains, and in dens and caves of the earth." In fact, the writer assures us that these people didn't even receive what God had promised: "These were all commended for their faith, yet none of them received what had been promised" (Hebrews 11:39 NIV).

To be a hero of faith, the pre-eminent aspect is, well, *faith*, not earthly accomplishments. Most of the heroes are praised here not for what they achieved, but for how they were afflicted. We value faith among leaders—heroes—in the Bible. What premium do we place on it for leaders in the contemporary Church? Yes, of course, faith is necessary for us and a fruit of the Spirit that we rightly haven't neglected in our teaching. However, it doesn't necessarily produce anything tangible or measurable for our churches, does it? In fact, the kind of faith we read about in Hebrews 11 might actually cause us to suffer loss—loss that is considered praiseworthy in Scripture. In spite of this, our pastors and leaders do all they can to *prevent* loss, in order to insure the continuation and survival of their own local expression of the body of Christ.

We teach from this passage about how wonderful and worthy of honor these heroes of faith are. However, we preachers—the very people exalting what faith is about and the kind of people who had it—do not live this kind of faith-walk ourselves. We just talk about it. And, somehow, just by talking about it with some degree of authority, we seem to be included in that notable company.

Strange how that happens.

So what do we do with this? What do we do with the writer of Hebrews and the attributes of the heroes of faith? What do we do with Paul and how he commended himself? I'm not advocating purposeful attempts at suffering and loss in order to attain a share of Paul's mantle of leadership. Nor should we induce self-destruction as a noble attempt to be included in that august list of the heroes of faith in Hebrews. What I am advocating, however, is a look at our hearts and what is commendable in ministry.

Please allow me to be blunt. All too often, we pastors and preachers have lifted up ourselves and our ministries. It seems as if we can't help talking about ourselves. It's what we do. It's who we are. We need to grow. We need to be more influential in our communities. We need to get people into our churches. We measure our success by what we have achieved. What would happen if we decided to not talk about our accomplishments in order to complete a project? What would happen if we didn't promote our ministries as a justification for raising money? I understand the justification. Money spent equals more people being reached for Jesus Christ. I get it. It makes sense.

However, it's not biblical. It's not what Paul or anyone else in the New Testament did in order to make their ministries "grow." I realize what a massive shift in thinking this would be for us, a paradigm adjustment so great that it seems almost impossible to comprehend. What scares me is that something so biblical seems so bizarre and foreign according to our modern ministry models, that what Paul considered commendable is a value so challenging that we would not even remotely consider doing it. What has happened to us? How did we depart so far from what Scripture values?

> *They didn't talk about their accomplishments in order to help their ministries grow. They just did ministry, serving others, plain and simple.*

Consider how Paul and the early disciples went about ministry. They were preachers of the gospel, teachers, pastors, apostles and workers of miracles. They labored with their own hands. They were faithful. They didn't talk about their accomplishments in order to help their ministries grow. They just did ministry, serving others, plain and simple. They suffered loss, for which they were lauded.

Would anybody you know want to join the ministry using these biblical criteria?

*The names of the individuals in this account have been changed.

Chapter Two

What Is Attractive?

"You have to have pace, you have to have high production values, you have to have interesting graphics, and you have to have attractive people."
~Brit Hume

"Come, see a man who told me all that I ever did. Can this be the Christ?"
~The Samaritan woman at the well

When I ask people what made Jesus attractive to the inhabitants of His culture, the most common response is, "He loved them."

Hard to disagree with that.

But how did He love them? Did He give them hugs? Well, we know, for example, that He forgave people.

The most famous example of Jesus' forgiveness is

when He cried from the cross, "Father, forgive them, for they know not what they do" (Luke 23:34a). Almost as well known is when He forgave the woman taken in adultery in John 8. After Jesus challenged the accusers to throw the first stone and none did, He said, "Neither do I condemn you; go, and from now on sin no more" (John 8:11b)

In Matthew 9:2b (Mark 2:5b), He forgave the paralytic before He healed him: "Take heart, my son; your sins are forgiven."

However, as important as these acts of forgiveness were—and in no way am I saying that they're not immensely significant—they weren't the primary reason why people were attracted to Jesus.

The people of Jesus' time were most often attracted by two things: His teaching and His acts of spiritual power, performed in His great compassion. Let's take a look at Luke 6:17-19:

> And he came down with them and stood on a level place, with a great crowd of his disciples and a great multitude of people from all Judea and Jerusalem and the seacoast of Tyre and Sidon, who came to hear him and to be healed of their diseases. And those who were troubled with unclean spirits were cured. And all the crowd sought to touch him, for power came out from him and healed them all.

There is evidence everywhere in the Gospels about Jesus attracting crowds through His miraculous acts of power. Mark 3:7-12 is a great example:

> Jesus withdrew with his disciples to the sea, and a great crowd followed, from Galilee and Judea and Jerusalem and Idumea and from beyond the Jordan and from around Tyre and Sidon. When the great crowd heard all that he was doing, they came to him. And he told his disciples to have a boat ready for him because of the crowd, lest they crush him, for he had healed many, so that all who had diseases pressed around him to touch him. And whenever the unclean spirits saw him, they fell down before him and cried out, "You are the Son of God." And he strictly ordered them not to make him known.

It's abundantly clear in the Gospels that what attracted people to Jesus were the extraordinary miracles He performed. However, those who say they were attracted by His love are correct. These were first and foremost acts of compassion and secondarily acts of power.

Then again, it's also true that the people were attracted by His teaching. Matthew 7:28-29 says, "And when Jesus finished these sayings, the crowds were astonished at his teaching, for he was teaching them as one who had authority, and not as their scribes."

Here is my point of departure with the evangelical church in the United States. We do a good job of teaching about Jesus, but we have almost completely ignored what made Jesus most attractive to people: His acts of supernatural power, fueled as they were by His kindness.

> *It's abundantly clear in the Gospels that what attracted people to Jesus were the extraordinary miracles He performed.*

Even when Jesus was being evangelistic without anyone being healed or delivered, spiritual gifts were in play. We see this in the account of His interaction with the Samaritan woman at the well in John 4. Consider verses 16-18:

> Jesus said to her, "Go, call your husband, and come here." The woman answered him, "I have no husband." Jesus said to her, "You are right in saying, 'I have no husband'; for you have had five husbands, and the one you now have is not your husband. What you have said is true."

The gift of the word of knowledge was operating through Jesus at that well in Samaria. He knew this woman's past. In fact, it is the functioning of this very gift that the woman referenced when she herself became an evangelist. "'Come, see a man who told me all that I ever did. Can this be the Christ?' They went out of the town and were coming to him" (John 4:29-30).

This method of attraction via acts of power continued to function in the ministry of the disciples and apostles after Jesus had ascended to heaven. What attracted the crowd on the Day of Pentecost? The outpouring of the Holy Spirit and accompanying miraculous works (Acts 2:41). Three thousand people came to the Lord that day.

What attracted people to Jesus through Peter's ministry at the Beautiful Gate? The healing of the lame man. This fellow was asking alms of those entering the temple, but he received a gift vastly more valuable than money. When Peter took him by the hand and told him to rise up and walk, his "feet and ankles were made strong." What effect did this have on those who knew about this beggar? "And they were filled with wonder and amazement at what had happened to him. While he clung to Peter and John, *all the people ran together to them in the portico called Solomon's, astounded*" (Acts 3:7, 10b-11 emphasis mine). In the presence of all those who had come to see the miracle that God had done, Peter was given the opportunity to preach.

Compassionate demonstrations of power continued in

the ministry of the church in Jerusalem. Signs and wonders were being done by the apostles, we are told, which caused them to be held in high esteem by the people. Sick people were being healed, even by Peter's shadow. Multitudes were coming to know the Lord (Acts 5:12-16).

When Philip went down to Samaria to proclaim the news about Jesus Christ, the working of miracles attracted people to Jesus through His ministry. People were set free from unclean spirits. The paralyzed and lame were healed. And, just like Peter after the healing of the man at the Gate Beautiful, Philip was given an opening to preach. "And the crowds with one accord paid attention to what was being said by Philip when they heard him and saw the signs that he did" (Acts 8:6).

Another opportunity to bring people to Jesus presented itself when Peter visited some saints at Lydda. A man named Aeneas had been bedridden for eight years and was paralyzed. "And Peter said to him, 'Aeneas, Jesus Christ heals you; rise and make your bed.' And immediately he rose. And all the residents of Lydda and Sharon saw him, and they turned to the Lord" (Acts 9:34-35).

Let's read that last sentence again. "And all the residents of Lydda and Sharon saw him (the man who had been paralyzed), and they turned to the Lord" (parenthesis added).

When a lady from nearby Joppa died, the disciples sent for Peter. This woman, Tabitha, was greatly loved, and those who knew her and her ministry were greatly distressed and weeping. Peter prayed for her.

> But Peter put them all outside, and knelt down and prayed; and turning to the body he said, "Tabitha, arise." And she opened her eyes, and when she saw Peter she sat up. And he gave her his hand and raised her up. Then calling the saints and widows, he presented her alive. *And it became known throughout all Joppa, and many believed in the Lord* (Acts 9:40-42, emphasis mine).

When Peter visited the house of Cornelius, it was a supernatural act of power that caused those who had gathered to give their lives to Jesus. It happened while Peter was preaching. The Holy Spirit "fell on all who heard the word." They began to speak in tongues and give praise to God. "Then Peter declared, 'Can anyone withhold water for baptizing these people, who have received the Holy Spirit just as we have?' And he commanded them to be baptized in the name of Jesus Christ. Then they asked him to remain for some days" (Acts 10:44-48).

These demonstrations of power were no different in the ministry of the apostle Paul. When Elymas the magician, who was opposing Paul's message, was temporarily struck blind through the power of the Holy Spirit, it so impressed the proconsul, Sergius Paulus, that he believed. "Then the proconsul believed, when he saw what had occurred, for he was astonished at the teaching of the Lord" (Acts 13:12). Please note that Sergius Paulus was "a man of intelligence." It was a supernatural act of power, along with Paul's teaching, that caused him to become a Christian.

The Philippian jailer was converted when he saw that an earthquake had not only opened all the doors of the prison, but everyone's bonds were unfastened as well.

> And the jailer called for lights and rushed in, and trembling with fear he fell down before Paul and Silas. Then he brought them out and said, "Sirs, what must I do to be saved?" And they said, "Believe in the Lord Jesus, and you will be saved, you and your household." And they spoke the word of the Lord to him and to all who were in his house. And he took them the same hour of the night and washed their wounds; and he was baptized at once, he and all his family (Acts 16:29-33).

People came to know the Lord in Ephesus through supernatural acts of power. Luke tells us that God did "extraordinary miracles by the hands of Paul." When the seven sons of Sceva tried to cast out some demons by "the Jesus, whom Paul proclaims," but the evil spirit said, "Jesus I know, and Paul I recognize, but who are you?"

and then proceeded to pummel those boys about the head and shoulders, the citizens of Ephesus took notice (Acts 19:11-16).

> And this became known to all the residents of Ephesus, both Jews and Greeks. And fear fell upon them all, and the name of the Lord Jesus was extolled. Also many of those who were now believers came, confessing and divulging their practices. And a number of those who had practiced magic arts brought their books together and burned them in the sight of all. And they counted the value of them and found it came to fifty thousand pieces of silver. So the word of the Lord continued to increase and prevail mightily (Acts 19:17-20).

It is impossible to ignore that the operation of supernatural gifts was the primary way that people came to Jesus Christ, both in the Gospels and in Acts.

To be fair, many began to follow Paul and Barnabas because of what was taught in the synagogues at Antioch and Iconium. There are no miraculous gifts in operation, apart from the opening of her heart by the Holy Spirit, in the conversion of Lydia. Nor are there any recorded in the accounts of Paul in Berea, Athens, or Corinth. I'm not advocating doing away with preaching and teaching.

Jesus taught. The disciples and apostles preached and taught. What I am advocating is, as we see biblically, the use of both.

My point of departure with the Church is that we have tried many different ways to attract people to Jesus at our gathering places. I understand them. I've been part of them, contributed to them and led them.

And now I question them.

However, you might say, "This is the Western culture that we're ministering in and trying to reach. People simply won't come to a church unless it offers the accoutrements we do."

I cannot argue that point. However, that isn't the primary issue. Yes, these are things we have done in our churches to attract people and perhaps should have, in God's will, done them. However, we shouldn't have done them while leaving the other unquestionably biblical things undone.

We have not been authentically scriptural in our ministries. We have tried to make Jesus attractive to people by using the methods and means of man.

> *We have not been authentically scriptural in our ministries. We have tried to make Jesus attractive to people by using the methods and means of man.*

Reaching the culture? The healing of individuals, without question, works cross-culturally as a gateway to see lives eternally impacted. Not only is this common sense, it is biblical. Culture made no difference to the people in the Book of Acts when people were being healed. Jew and Gentile alike, from different parts of the world where the apostles and disciples were ministering, responded to the healing and deliverance of individuals.

The reason, I think, that the Western Church has shied away from the gifts of the Spirit is because of excesses. I understand that. There have been excesses. However, there have been excesses in teaching and preaching, too. We haven't stopped teaching and preaching because of these excesses, have we? There's more going on here than that excuse alone, apparently. Is it lack of faith? Is it lack of power?

I don't know. However, I advocate making a relatively simple change: start praying for the sick and the spiritually oppressed when we gather. Start asking for God's power. How should it be done? Biblically. If we look at how Jesus and His disciples ministered healing and deliverance in the Gospels and the Book of Acts, we don't see any showmanship, fooferah

> *We should never use the miraculous acts of God to promote our ministries.*

or excesses—just simple, direct, sensible, compassionate ministry. This kind of ministry, as far as the Bible indicates, doesn't require anything but the act of doing it in faith. Jesus is the Healer and Deliverer, we aren't. We pray—or, as we see in the biblical examples, we speak—and healing and deliverance happen. The results are up to Him. However, it's certain that no miracles whatsoever will be done if we don't act, if we don't pray.

And, when miracles begin to happen, we must keep our mouths shut. We must not exalt ourselves. We should never use the miraculous acts of God to promote our ministries. Let the people who have been healed and delivered talk about them. Sometimes, Jesus told people not to do even that (Luke 5:12-15, 8:49-56; Mark 7:31-37). What we never hear Jesus or His followers say is how someone had been healed or delivered through their ministries. We do find one instance where the seventy—or seventy-two—who had been sent out to go before Jesus, proclaim the kingdom of God and to heal, came back to Him rejoicing that demons were subject to them in His name. He didn't rebuke them but told them not to rejoice in their victory over spiritual darkness because there was something of far greater importance: that they knew Him (Luke 10:17-20).

If we use God's miraculous gifts to promote and grow our ministries, we have fallen. My opinion is that this is one of the reasons God has withheld these acts of supernatural power from us. He's waiting for us to have a biblical reversal in how we view ministry. Is it possible that we have been too concerned about placing a list of accomplishments, figuratively speaking, under our church letterhead? Is it possible that, in our hearts, we would want people to be healed, not only because we're concerned about them, but also because it would draw people to what we're doing in *our* particular ministry?

Why can't we keep quiet about what the Lord has done through us or through our ministries? What would happen to our churches if wonderful acts of God were happening and we *didn't* intentionally leverage them for church growth—would we have to close our doors because no one would show up? No. If God was doing dramatic acts of power in and through us and the people we work with, the results would be the same as we see in the Book of Acts—individuals turning to God and glorifying Him.

> *People were and are drawn to Jesus by His teaching and through His amazing acts of healing, deliverance and transformation, driven by His compassionate love.*

Would they then attend your church?

You shouldn't care. It's not about you. It's not about your church or your ministry. It's about Jesus and people coming to know Him, plain and simple.

It would be refreshing—no, it would be honorable and, I contend, God-pleasing—for us to no longer promote our ministries by talking about what God was doing through them. Miracles speak quite loudly for themselves, as we clearly learn from the examples in Scripture.

People were and are drawn to Jesus by His teaching and through His amazing acts of healing, deliverance and transformation, driven by His compassionate love. These are what make Him attractive.

I propose that we put our hand to the rudder and begin to swing the ship of the Church around and spend far less time, expenditure and staff on making our facilities and services culturally appealing and return to the biblical model of what made Jesus so appealing: His supernatural, healing power, based on His loving compassion and desire to honor His Father, not because He desired to "build" a ministry.

If we do this, I maintain that we will then be navigating in the God-honoring, full-sail current of where the Bible specifies our ministries should be—although we'll have to deny fame and importance in order to stay there. And shouldn't that be acceptable to us?

Chapter Three

What Is Presentable?

"For he who is least among you all is the one who is great."
~Jesus Christ

"God chose what is weak in the world to shame the strong."
~Paul, the apostle

I've always loved those verses from First Corinthians, the ones that tell us that God chooses the weak and foolish:

> For consider your calling, brothers: not many of you were wise according to worldly standards, not many were powerful, not many were of noble birth. But God chose what is foolish in the world

> to shame the wise; God chose what is weak in the world to shame the strong; God chose what is low and despised in the world, even things that are not, to bring to nothing things that are, so that no human being might boast in the presence of God (1 Corinthians 1:26-29).

Maybe it's because it appeals to my sense of fairness and love for the underdog. Maybe it's because I'm not particularly wise or powerful. Regardless, I've been so happily amazed when, down through the years, those who are down and dirty get their lives turned around by Jesus. It just seems to be so honoring to Jesus, so right.

I'm sure that's why I was so concerned about what I was hearing the speaker say that day, why it was so disturbing.

I was attending a leadership conference presented by a very successful and influential seeker-sensitive ministry. The pastor was talking about how churches needed to have the best possible people in their visible ministries. I understood this. My pastor at the time had explained to the church more than once over the years how embarrassing it was to bring a friend to church when Sister Helen, who was playing the piano, was all thumbs—and the awkwardness that resulted. Sure. I agreed. It made sense. We needed talented musicians up front. What caught my attention, however, was when the speaker said, "And don't use the verses from the first

> *Can people who are, to use Paul's words, not powerful, not of noble birth, weak, low and despised in the world, be used in the visible ministries in the Church? And if not, why not?*

chapter of First Corinthians as an excuse for using someone unsuitable."

As I said, it made sense. But didn't it fly directly in the face of Scripture—indeed; didn't it seem contrary to the heart of God, who always seems to honor the least among us? So the question I would ask is this: Has something gone wrong in the Church when we tell our people to ignore Bible passages in favor of a ministry stance that really has no biblical backing? Can people who are, to use Paul's words, not powerful, not of noble birth, weak, low and despised in the world, be used in the visible ministries in the Church?

And if not, why not?

****

I understand the desire and need to have your place look presentable when guests arrive—whether it's a home, a store front or a church building. I also understand getting dressed up, cleaned up and looking one's best when company comes. But I think we need to be extremely careful when we translate that presentability to the attractiveness of people, their ability to buy good clothing and their natural talents, because of what the Bible teaches us about how to regard the poor and disadvantaged among us. James gave us a strong warning in his letter.

> My brothers, show no partiality as you hold the faith in our Lord Jesus Christ, the Lord of glory. For if a man wearing a gold ring and fine clothing comes into your assembly, and a poor man in shabby clothing also comes in, and if you pay attention to the one who wears the fine clothing and say, "You sit here in a good place," while you say to the poor man, "You stand over there," or, "Sit down at my feet," have you not then made distinctions among yourselves and become judges with evil thoughts? Listen, my beloved brothers, has not God chosen those who are poor in the world to be rich in faith and heirs of the kingdom, which he has promised to those who love him? But you have dishonored the poor man. Are not the rich the ones who oppress you, and the ones who drag you into court? Are they not the ones who blaspheme

> the honorable name by which you were called? If you really fulfill the royal law according to the Scripture, "You shall love your neighbor as yourself," you are doing well. But if you show partiality, you are committing sin and are convicted by the law as transgressors. For whoever keeps the whole law but fails in one point has become accountable for all of it
> (James 2:1-10).

We have applied those verses to how we treat people when they visit our churches, rightfully so, but do these verses apply to those who are to be in the visible ministries in our churches? If not, why not? The reason this is so difficult for us is because of the way our church services are structured. James, the brother of Jesus, praises the poor in the above verses, the ones who might not be able to dress as well as some of us, who might not be as attractive, who may not be as gifted.

Let's look at what Paul says in 1 Corinthians, chapter twelve.

> The eye cannot say to the hand, "I have no need of you," nor again the head to the feet, "I have no need of you." On the contrary, the parts of the body that seem to be weaker are indispensable, and on

> those parts of the body that we think less honorable we bestow the greater honor, and our unpresentable parts are treated with greater modesty, which our more presentable parts do not require. But God has so composed the body, giving greater honor to the part that lacked it, that there may be no division in the body, but that the members may have the same care for one another (21-25).

I contend that the above passage has very little meaning in the evangelical church today. We haven't bestowed greater honor on the less honorable parts of the body. We bestow honor on the most presentable parts, in perfect contradiction to the Scripture. In fact, due to our religious structures, the idea of bestowing honor on our "unpresentable parts" is one that we simply can't comprehend. We would have no idea about how to do that.

Isn't God in the business of using what is small and unnoticed? Doesn't it seem that He exults in doing great things through insignificance? Isn't this what we tell people from our pulpits?

A great example is Gideon and his small army. Gideon had gathered some men to fight against the Midianites and Amalekites. Apparently he had done his recruiting too well. The Lord told him to whittle down his forces. Twenty-two thousand soldiers were sent home, leaving ten thousand. There were still too many, according to the Lord, who told Gideon to reduce his numbers even more. When it was all said and done, Gideon had three hundred men remaining. Three hundred. He started out with around thirty-two thousand (Judges 7:1-8). The Lord's battle strategy to defeat the enemy? Break earthen jars. Blow trumpets. Hold up torches and yell. "When they blew the 300 trumpets, the LORD set every man's sword against his comrade and against all the army" (Judges 7:22a). The seemingly weak actions of Gideon's forces defeated an army that had numbers "like locusts in abundance" (7:12). Numbers had little to do with the victory the Lord brought that day.

Another example is the widow who ministered to Elijah, with her small portion of oil and meal. The Lord told the prophet to go to Zarephath, where he would find a widow who would feed him. She did provide a meal for him, but she told him that she had only "a handful of flour in a jar and a little oil in a jug" (1 Kings 17:12). In fact, before Elijah arrived, she was getting ready to prepare it, have a small meal with her son and die. However, Elijah told her that her little portion would be enough. "Make me a little cake of it," he told her. "For thus says the LORD, the God of Israel, 'The jar of flour shall not be spent, and the jug of oil shall not be empty, until the day that the LORD sends rain upon the earth.' And she went and did as Elijah said. And she and he and her household ate for many days. The jar of flour was not spent, neither did the jug of oil become empty, according to the word of the LORD that he spoke by Elijah" (1 Kings 17:14-16).

It was an impoverished, starving widow, with her handful of flour and meager amount of oil, for whom the Lord performed a wondrous act of provision.

And consider Israel. She wasn't the biggest or the best. She was the least.

> It was not because you were more in number than any other people that the LORD set his love on you and chose you, for you were the fewest of all peoples, but it is because the LORD loves you and is keeping the oath that he swore to your fathers, that the LORD has brought you out with a mighty hand and redeemed you from the house of slavery, from the hand of Pharaoh king of Egypt
> (Deuteronomy 7:7-8).

The Lord could have chosen a large, notable people through which to give the Law, raise up prophets, do amazing works of power and, most importantly, create a lineage through which our beloved Messiah would come. He didn't. He chose, as He said, the fewest of all peoples.

David, who would be king, was almost forgotten by his family when Samuel came to find one he could anoint to lead Israel. David, the greatest king in the history of Israel, a man after God's heart, was forgotten out in the pasture. And there is Bethlehem. I love this beautiful prophecy concerning that little-known town:

> But you, Bethlehem Ephrathah, though you are small among the clans of Judah, out of you will come for me one who will be ruler over Israel, whose origins are from of old, from ancient times
> (Micah 5:2 NIV).

Even God Himself chose to be least, being born among the animals, to a poor family in Bethlehem, a location that was off the world's map of significance.

What about Nazareth, where Jesus, the Son of God, grew up, that town of bad reputation and crude speech? Nothing good could come from there, could it?

There are more examples. The widow's mite:

> Jesus sat down opposite the place where the offerings were put and watched the crowd putting their money into the temple treasury. Many rich people threw in large amounts. But a poor widow came and put in two very small copper coins, worth only a fraction of a penny. Calling his disciples to him, Jesus said, "I tell you the truth, this

poor widow has put more into the treasury than all the others. They all gave out of their wealth; but she, out of her poverty, put in everything—all she had to live on." (Mark 12:41-44 NIV).

And consider the very familiar account from John 6:1-14, of the young boy's lunch, which fed five thousand people. Five loaves and two fish, barely enough for one family. The provision that day was the result of being connected to *Jesus'* family. Inadequate earthly resources mean nothing to Him. He, the limitless One, rejoices in using what we consider limited.

Isn't this the point that Jesus was trying to make when He said this about what true greatness is among us? "For he who is least among you all is the one who is great." (Luke 9:48b).

We have turned this concept—this biblical concept—on its head in our churches. We believe the Lord will do this outside our church walls, but we don't want it happening in our visible ministries inside the church building, with people who are serving at our services. The question I want to ask is: Why? Why can't we believe that the Lord could use what is small and unimportant in our church services, the way we believe He can do that everywhere else?

We know the answer. We want people to like us and our churches. We want unbelievers to come to our services, and we don't want anything to be awkward or to "go wrong." Visitors will like us if we're presentable in a contemporary way, according to our way of thinking. The problem is that our way of thinking isn't God's way of thinking. In fact, it is 180 degrees from His thoughts. We have negated the Lord's supernatural ability to take people and circumstances of little significance and use them to change people's lives and thereby glorify Himself.

We can't have Sister Helen playing the piano and making a mistake because it's embarrassing. Why is it embarrassing? It's embarrassing because the focus is on it being a performance, not a ministry to God

> *We have negated the Lord's supernatural ability to take people and circumstances of little significance and use them to change people's lives and thereby glorify Himself.*

and no one else. However, what if we were in a venue where the emphasis had little to do with talent and more to do with an authentic heart for God, with godly seeking and very little concern for the talent used to express that heart and that seeking?

Can the mistakes people make when they're singing be off-putting? Sure. Can it interrupt our worship? Yes. However, when this happens, we should join in and help the person by singing along on key. When this happens, we learn how to be mature, realize the preciousness of the humanity involved, worship in that godly knowledge and then move on to the next song. Then *we* offer a song. However, in our current traditional Western church structure—which is not a biblical structure—this seems beyond comprehension.

How important is the relationship to skill and worship, biblically? I'm not saying it is unimportant. Nor do I maintain that talented musicians should not feel free to sing or play when believers gather to worship. However, they shouldn't be the only ones who are singing or playing.

The focus on music in worship that we see in Scripture is different from our focus today. Musicians were used when prophets spoke (1 Chronicles 25:1), when battles were won (2 Chronicles 20:27-28), when burnt offerings were offered on the altar (2 Chronicles 29:25-28) and when the wall of Jerusalem was dedicated (Nehemiah 12:27). These musicians had one purpose and one purpose only: to offer praise—and often supplication, as we read the Psalms—to the living God. They weren't—or at least, they shouldn't have been—concerned at all with what someone thought about their musicianship or if it was a bit embarrassing because Uncle Moishe was all thumbs.

The ministry of music, according to what Paul says in Ephesians, does have another helpful aspect. We sing in order to minister to the believers in our midst. "... addressing one another in psalms and hymns and spiritual songs, singing and making melody to the Lord with all your heart..." (Ephesians 5:19). We are to address "one another in psalms and hymns and spiritual songs." What this means is that we—we—are to minister to one another or to the group as a whole by singing songs of faith and encouragement. How much talent would this require? Not much. What it does require is a heart that is concerned about the needs of the individuals in the group.

Colossians 3:16 says much the same thing about the requirement to be ready to minister to one another:

> Let the word of Christ dwell in you richly, teaching and admonishing one another in all wisdom, singing psalms and hymns and spiritual songs, with thankfulness in your hearts to God.

Here Paul emphasizes the necessity of having the word of Christ dwelling in us richly, in order to teach and admonish one another. Not just the pastor. Not just the staff. Not just a couple of people. This kind of ministry would require all of us studying Scripture and preparing in advance to have a word or a song that would minister in a loving, helpful way.

However, serving the Lord and one another in this strength-engendering, biblical fashion is so foreign to our minds that the accomplishment of it seems incomprehensible to us.

How different is what we see in Scripture and what

we see today concerning how we view music? Here is an extraordinary example, taken from the life of Jesus Himself.

> Now as they were eating, Jesus took bread, and after blessing it broke it and gave it to the disciples, and said, "Take, eat; this is my body." And he took a cup, and when he had given thanks he gave it to them, saying, "Drink of it, all of you, for this is my blood of the covenant, which is poured out for many for the forgiveness of sins. I tell you I will not drink again of this fruit of the vine until that day when I drink it new with you in my Father's kingdom." And when they had sung a hymn, they went out to the Mount of Olives (Matthew 26:26-30).

This is, without controversy, one of the most important events in Scripture—the institution of the Lord's Supper. I was taken aback when I realized the musical component of this event: They sang a hymn. One hymn. I wondered what kind of music we would have planned for an event of such monumental importance. Apparently, as far as Jesus was concerned, this one song was sufficient, both for Him and for His disciples.

How good was this singing? Did they all sing on key?

We're not told. How worshipful was this time? We don't know. Each one of those men was required to worship God from their hearts. Whether they did this or not was known only to them and to God. The worship that evening had little or nothing to do with talent.

****

In addition to worship, our modern view of children's involvement in ministry has also departed from Scripture. Our present structure denies the possibility for children to participate in ministry, the kind of ministry the Bible indicates, where they are required to bring something to the meeting. "What then, brothers? When you come together, each one has a hymn, a lesson, a revelation, a tongue, or an interpretation. Let all things be done for building up" (1 Corinthians 14:26). This scripture doesn't specify that children should be present, but it doesn't say that they should be absent, either. If our children grow up in this

> *Truthfully, I would prefer having a child pray for me. Their minds and belief systems are uncluttered. They pray in simple faith, believing God. We should include them in our meetings, not exclude them.*

kind of biblical ministry, however, there will be a time when they will be old and mature enough to participate. Will there be uncomfortable, awkward times when children are present? Yes. There are those moments in all phases of childrearing, but we don't stop having children because of them. It is actually possible to have children with adults at our gatherings and believe that the Holy Spirit could be at work in their lives, too. Truthfully, I would prefer having a child pray for me. Their minds and belief systems are uncluttered. They pray in simple faith, believing God. We should include them in our meetings, not exclude them.

What follows is an amazing example of this inclusion, written by the wonderfully radical missionary, Ted Olbrich, who serves in Cambodia:

> I had all the key leaders, Elders, District Supervisors, Divisional Superintendents and board members, 134 people, come to Phnom Penh for meetings. I asked them, "If I got very sick, who do you think I'd really want to pray for me?" They looked at each other and finally one ventured, "Mak Sou?" I said she'd be on the top of the list, but not the one I would choose for maximum power. They looked a little shocked and someone guessed, "Pastor Peter?" "Umm, again, near the top but not my 'powerhouse.'"

They were dumbfounded. Finally, after looking around the room, in virtual unison they blurted out, "Who then?" I said, "Mathay!" Their mouths dropped open, and they gave me this, "You've got to be kidding!" look. I explained, "No, I'm serious!" I couldn't blame them for their shock, but most of them had not seen Mathay in action. I had. Mathay is a Down syndrome boy of about 16.

I doubt if you could measure his I.Q. The locals call him stupid because he doesn't speak much and is commonly known as "Monkey Boy." He does kind of act like a monkey, because as an infant he was raised in the jungle by monkeys for from two to six months, depending upon whose story you believe. You see, his parents were fishermen along the Great Lake, and the village people would dry fish in the sun for future sale. Large monkeys would like to sneak in and steal the fish. One day, in 1994, the village was overrun by Khmer Rouge. Mathay was just a month or two old when his parents were killed. The surviving villagers ran into the jungle for safety. They did not return until the next day. They could not find Mathay so assumed he'd been taken and killed. Months later, poachers were hunting in the forest, and they shot a large female monkey. When they went to pick her up they found this human baby. Not knowing what to do, they took the infant to the local Buddhist Temple. The monks tried to raise him for several years, but determined that since he couldn't speak, that he'd been "monkeyized": lived with the monkeys so long he'd become one. So, they just let Mathay run free. They'd put food out for him, he'd disappear for days into the jungle and eventually come back. This went on until 1999 when one of our pastors heard about Mathay. He went and brought him into our Toule Kok Orphan Home where he has been ever since. In the early days, he'd scamper up trees and sleep in the branches. Gradually, as he grew, he became too big for such gymnastics, but he does love to dance and play like a monkey.

Ever since the Holy Spirit fell on the entire group of orphans at the Toule Kok church/home on a Friday evening in March of

2000, they have gathered for prayer at 7:00 p.m. each Friday night. Mathay was in that group. Most Fridays Mathay will be running around like a monkey, poking his neighbor, acting mischievous, until some deep spiritual need arises. How he picks this up can only be explained by God. He will chasten anyone who does not go into earnest prayer, and he falls to his hands and knees and weeps before the Lord until the Spirit lifts the burden. I have never seen such intense prayer from any person anywhere in the world! (From the June 2009 update on the Foursquare Children of Promise website.)

Let's keep in mind that Jesus was indignant—very displeased—with His disciples when they attempted to prevent children from being present at His gatherings.

> And they were bringing children to him that he might touch them, and the disciples rebuked them. But when Jesus saw it, he was indignant and said to them, "Let the children come to me; do not hinder them, for to such belongs the kingdom of God. Truly, I say to you, whoever does not receive the kingdom of God like a child

shall not enter it." And he took them in his arms and blessed them, laying his hands on them (Mark 10:13-16).

I find it fascinating that Jesus said this in the context of a gathering in His presence. The kingdom of God belongs to such as these, He said. Whoever doesn't receive the kingdom of God like a child shall not enter it, He said. Sounds pretty important. Sounds like we have something to learn from children. Why do we think we shouldn't have them around? Yes, they're too often noisy and unfocused. However, children witnessing their parents and other sincere adult Christians authentically praying, seeking and worshiping God provides profound opportunities for them to have life-changing, spiritual encounters. We should encourage this, not attempt to prevent it—like the disciples did.

The more I learn about how Jesus wants gatherings done in His presence, the more it seems that He actually likes things "messy"—messy in the sense that love and maturity are required from us and are more crucial than order and control so that everything runs smoothly. How far have we strayed from what Jesus considers important?

****

How should we view the "unpresentable" brother or sister, who isn't "pretty enough" or "talented enough" to be involved in visible ministry in our churches? This issue disappears. Physical appearance, clothing, education and even talent have little to do with the bringing of the kind of spiritual ministry that 1 Corinthians 14:26, Ephesians 5:19 and Colossians 3:16 bring to us. It's all about one's heart. It's all about one's desire to serve others. It's about serving others in a biblical way, in a meeting-together way, where a person, regardless of his or her presentability, can minister in as important a way as...a pastor can.

The response to this may be, "Just because this kind of person doesn't have the opportunity to serve—except perhaps as an usher or a helper—in our services, that doesn't mean he or she can't minister outside the church services themselves."

> *The modern evangelical church service has become a presentation of talent.*

Well, what then does this say to those who attend our churches about our services, in light of 1 Corinthians 14:26, Ephesians 5:19 and Colossians 3:16? What shall we say to James? And what does this say to those who are less "presentable"? Are we telling them by our actions that only those who are beautiful, talented, educated or handsome have a chance of ministering in any significant way—the way the big boys do—in our church gatherings?

The modern evangelical church service has become a presentation of talent. There is nothing wrong with the use of talent. It is given by God. However, we have lifted up talent, looks, education—presentability—and have disallowed those less favored. David would have remained out in the pasture with the sheep; Gideon abandoned at the winepress. The widow of Zarephath would have starved with her handful of meal. Shepherds would have been left wondering if they were worthy to share their amazing news of the revelation of God's glory. Aged Anna and Simeon would have died without speaking those wondrous words of prophecy about the Lord Jesus. Mary Magdalene, who had seven demons, would have withheld her startling glad tidings. The Western evangelical church has limited itself. It has limited itself by using worldly definitions of what is presentable. There are so many people of "insignificance" through whom God may wish to speak, but we have denied them the opportunity. This has weakened us. This has impoverished us. Let us return to the biblical truth: when we are weak, then we are strong.

Chapter Four

What Is Wealth?

*"Nothing is more fallacious than wealth.
It is a hostile comrade, a domestic enemy."*
~John Chrysostom

*"To be clever enough to get all the money,
one must be stupid enough to want it."*
~Gilbert K. Chesterton

Because I'm a pastor, I'm greatly concerned, as all pastors are, about the state of the spiritual maturity of individuals in the Church. We teach people to take time to pray, to read the Bible, to have a disciplined devotional life, as we should. However, I'm beginning to wonder if there is an issue that in some ways undermines those admonitions, one to which we're essentially blind.

That issue is wealth. Possessions. Money. To explain

what I mean, let's look at Jesus' explanation of the parable of the sower.

> Hear then the parable of the sower: When anyone hears the word of the kingdom and does not understand it, the evil one comes and snatches away what has been sown in his heart. This is what was sown along the path. As for what was sown on rocky ground, this is the one who hears the word and immediately receives it with joy, yet he has no root in himself, but endures for a while, and when tribulation or persecution arises on account of the word, immediately he falls away. As for what was sown among thorns, this is the one who hears the word, but the cares of the world and the deceitfulness of riches choke the word, and it proves unfruitful. As for what was sown on good soil, this is the one who hears the word and understands it. He indeed bears fruit and yields, in one case a hundredfold, in another sixty, and in another thirty (Matthew 13:18-23).

We trivialize this parable when our exegesis causes us to think that what Jesus teaches here narrowly concerns the preaching of the gospel to unbelievers or only one event in our lives, our initial salvation. This teaching is much broader than that. It should apply to every instance when the Sower speaks to our hearts. Jesus' instruction in this parable becomes much more vital when we are humble enough to accept that it applies to all of us *all the time*, whenever He challenges us about the nature of the kingdom of God, when He sows His word into our lives. However, as the parable teaches, if trouble begins to occur because we try to follow His difficult word, we may fall away from that truth and, possibly, from Him, if the trial is severe, like what happened to the second seed. The same holds true for the seed sown among thorns, the third seed. It isn't that we haven't ever had fruit in our lives—it's that this particular word from Jesus, at this particular time in our growth in Him, is choked out.

What is it that causes the word of the kingdom to be choked in this third seed?

First of all, Jesus says, the cares of the world. These are not necessarily evil things. They are more often morally neutral things, even what we would consider good things. Security. Safety. Comfort. Concern about family. Earthly responsibilities and commitments. We may rejoice and accept at first a word about giving up something in our lives, some aspect of self-denial that His Spirit speaks to us about. However, as we begin to reflect on the possibility of acting on it, the breath-taking excitement of sacrificially serving Jesus fades in the light of everyday reality. The fruit of the word that Jesus spoke to us by His Spirit is choked out.

This happened when the Lord began to stir my heart about re-entering the mission field. My wife, Laurie, and I experienced a lot of joy as we considered the prospect of leaving, again, our homeland with its accompanying security and comfort in order to minister to those overseas. However, missionaries rarely just pick up and leave when the Lord calls them to service. There are matters to attend to. Money to be raised. Preparations to be made. It takes time, and soon the initial excitement of going to another country may begin to fade.

One day, I was downstairs in our home with nothing much to do. It was wintertime, the fireplace was on, radiating comfortable, inviting warmth, and the remote control for the TV was in my hand. Suddenly, a thought went through my head: "Why on earth would you ever want to leave this?" It was a great question, but I don't think it was God who was doing the asking. I'll be transparent here. I've asked that very same question myself many times and wrestled with leaving the safety, security and comfort that most of us enjoy here in the United States. The cares and affairs of the world have threatened to choke out the word that Jesus, the Sower, placed in my heart.

The second thing that chokes out the fruit of God's word in this parable is "the deceitfulness of riches." Riches, according to Jesus as He explained this parable, are deceitful. So what should I do with this? Should I say, "I'm rich (by the world's standards), but there's no way I could be deceived by that wealth?" Or should I be willing to humbly admit that Jesus is indeed right, and that it's possible that I have in some way been deceived by riches?

The wise choice is to admit that what Jesus says is accurate: Riches are deceitful, and it's very possible that I have been deceived by them.

In addition, since I'm a citizen of the United States, one of the richest countries in the history of the world, I'm very concerned about what Jesus says about being wealthy in these verses:

> *Or should I be willing to humbly admit that Jesus is indeed right, and that it's possible that I have in some way been deceived by riches?*

> Truly, I say to you, only with difficulty will a rich person enter the kingdom of heaven. Again I tell you, it is easier for a camel to go through the eye of a needle than for a rich person to enter the kingdom of God (Matthew 19:23-24).

A camel going through the eye of a needle. I know that Jesus goes on to say that all things are possible with God, but still—that sounds just a bit—difficult.

Jesus isn't talking about going to heaven when He teaches us about entering the kingdom of heaven here—

which He also refers to as the kingdom of God in other places—since we know that one is saved through faith and grace alone. He's talking about entering the kingdom of God, a reality that is both present and future, initiated by His coming—and by that He must mean entering into a place of ruling and being ruled—as one would do in a kingdom. Ruling how? Well, we know what He said about the kingdom in the Beatitudes. Blessed are the poor, Jesus taught in Luke, and blessed are the poor in spirit, in Matthew, for the kingdom of heaven is theirs. Both require a humble dependence upon God, and an admission that we desperately need Him. Being desperate for God is really difficult to do when one is not dependent, but independent, self-reliant, not God-reliant. Apparently, humble reliance on God and an admission of how poor we really are, is how one accesses the kingdom of God.

That's difficult to do when one is wealthy. Going-through-the-eye-of-a-needle difficult.

Is what Jesus says about the word of the Sower being choked out by the cares of the world applicable to our churches? Is it possible that the Lord might speak a challenging word to us that we would ignore—it

> *Humble reliance on God and an admission of how poor we really are, is how one accesses the kingdom of God.*

could be choked out—because of the cares of the world and by the deceitfulness of riches? It is not impossible that we've been deceived by riches, not only in our own personal lives, but in the lives of our structural organizations.

Are our churches rich? Have they prevented us from entering into a place of rulership with God? If they have, what Jesus teaches may help us understand why. We are rich. The nature of the organization causes us to endeavor to be, not dependent on God, but sufficient in and of ourselves. We have salary expenses, insurance premiums and mortgage payments to make. We have to make them, if the local institution is to continue. We have to make them whether God comes through or not.

The incident that preceded this camel-going-through-the-eye-of-a-needle statement by Jesus is also troubling.

> And behold, a man came up to him, saying, "Teacher, what good deed must I do to have eternal life?" And he said to him, "Why do you ask me about what is good? There is only one who is good. If you would enter life, keep the commandments." He said to him, "Which ones?" And Jesus said, "You shall not murder, You shall not commit adultery, You shall not steal, You shall not bear false witness, Honor your father and mother, and, You shall love your neighbor as yourself." The young man said to him,

> "All these I have kept. What do I still lack?" Jesus said to him, "If you would be perfect, go, sell what you possess and give to the poor, and you will have treasure in heaven; and come, follow me." When the young man heard this he went away sorrowful, for he had great possessions (Matthew 19:16-22).

It should bother you, too, I think. I know that we often teach that this was a specific requirement that Jesus gave to this man and that we don't necessarily need to take this as a general command to all of us. Granted. But we should ask this question: What would I do if Jesus *did* come up to me today and say, "If you want to follow Me, sell all you possess and give it to the poor"? What would my response be? Would I really be willing to sell everything I possess and give it away? I don't know about you, but that would be very, very difficult for me to do. (Difficult. Why am I thinking of camels and the eyes of needles again?) I'm pretty sure my response would begin with, "But, Lord, isn't there some other way to follow You?"

And so I see that Jesus was entirely correct—not that He needs me to verify His accuracy regarding the truth—when He said that it was very difficult for a rich man to enter the kingdom of God. It's true for me.

A bit challenging, isn't it?

Here are two other things that bother me about this

portion of Scripture. Jesus told the man that if he were to sell all he possessed and give to the poor, he would have treasure in heaven. Whether or not we consider this requirement Jesus makes just for this man or for us, the truth about storing up treasure in heaven is applicable for all of us.

Jesus says much the same thing in Luke 12:32-34:

> Fear not, little flock, for it is your Father's good pleasure to give you the kingdom. Sell your possessions, and give to the needy. Provide yourselves with moneybags that do not grow old, with a treasure in the heavens that does not fail, where no thief approaches and no moth destroys. For where your treasure is, there will your heart be also.

If we were to sell all we possess and give it to the poor, we would have treasure in heaven. I have to ask myself, "Why isn't this important to me? Why isn't it important that I have treasure in

> *What would we say if Jesus came to us, as pastors and leaders, and made the same requirement? Sell the building. Sell the assets. Give it to the poor. You'll have treasure in heaven. Then all of you come follow Me.*

heaven—a treasure that will be eternal? Why is it more important to me to have treasure here on earth, wealth that is so very temporary, according to Jesus?"

I struggle mightily with this question. I'm not happy with my answer. I tend to value my treasures here on earth more than I value having treasure in heaven. It's as simple as that. I am amazingly earthly minded.

The second thing that bothers me is giving it all to the poor. Giving it to the church, I understand. Giving it to a ministry organization, I understand. But if I gave it all to the poor, I wouldn't be building anything, would I? I wouldn't be advancing anything, it seems. It just seems like giving this way would be—should I really admit this?—a poor—pardon the pun—ministry investment.

Now explode that out for a larger picture that includes our churches. What would we say if Jesus came to us, as pastors and leaders, and made the same requirement? Sell the building. Sell the assets. Give it to the poor. You'll have treasure in heaven. Then all of you come follow Me.

****

One recent winter night, the area in which we live experienced a relatively big snowfall—about ten inches. As my wife, Laurie, and I were reading in bed that Saturday evening, I turned to her and asked, "What do you think is the primary concern of our pastor friends here in town concerning services tomorrow morning?"

Without hesitation she said—well, wait a minute. If you're a pastor, what would *your* main concern have been?

Laurie responded by saying, "The offering."

I agreed.

Then, I asked, "Isn't there something wrong with that?" Isn't there something wrong with our institution when our primary concern is funding?

****

Have you ever played the lottery? I have. I've prayed that I would win, so I could give most of it away to the church and the needy. I've never won. In so doing, I ignored this advice from 1 Timothy:

> Now there is great gain in godliness with contentment, for we brought nothing into the world, and we cannot take anything out of the world. But if we have food and clothing, with these we will be content. But those who desire to be rich fall into temptation, into a snare, into many senseless and harmful desires that plunge people into ruin and destruction. For the love of money is a root of all kinds of evils. It is through this craving that some have wandered away from the faith and pierced

themselves with many pangs
(1 Timothy 6:6-10).

"Those who desire to be rich fall into temptation, into a snare, into many senseless and harmful desires that plunge people into ruin and destruction," Paul teaches. Who desires to be rich in this country? We all do. So does that mean that we have plunged ourselves into ruin and destruction? Nah, couldn't be. Couldn't be us, couldn't be *me*.

Could it?

I wonder, sometimes, if we in the Western Church are in more trouble than we think we are. If we have indeed been deceived by riches, I believe the answer is yes; we are wading at eye level through deep weeds.

Jesus said something in the sixth chapter of Matthew that troubles me greatly:

> Do not store up for yourselves treasures on earth, where moth and rust destroy, and where thieves break in and steal. But store up for yourselves treasures in heaven, where moth and rust do not destroy, and where thieves do not break in and steal. For where your treasure is, there your heart will be also. The eye is the lamp of the body. If your eyes are good, your whole body will be full of light. But if your eyes are bad, your whole body will be full

of darkness. If then the light within you is darkness, how great is that darkness! No one can serve two masters. Either he will hate the one and love the other, or he will be devoted to the one and despise the other. You cannot serve both God and Money (Matthew 6:19-24 NIV).

Let's look at the context. Jesus begins by telling us not to store up treasures for ourselves here on earth. Already we're in a predicament, because that is exactly what we tend to do. However, following His admonition about storing up treasure He makes this statement about good eyes and bad eyes. If our eyes are good, He says, our

> *If we want to be His disciples—if we pastors and leaders want to be His disciples—we must give up from our hearts all the financial investment we've made into our churches and be ready, at any moment, to sell all and give to the poor.*

bodies will be full of light. But if our eyes are bad—a Hebrew idiom for being greedy—our bodies will be full of darkness. Then, this warning: "If the light within you is darkness, how great is that darkness!" Next Jesus tells us that we cannot serve two masters, that we cannot serve God and money.

There's something here that makes me nervous. Contextually, we cannot refute that the topic in this portion of scripture is money, wealth, or treasure—the teaching begins with this subject and ends with it. But why is this warning about our eyes being good or bad and the light within us being darkness—*here*? Is it possible that Jesus is warning us that if we do not store up treasure in heaven and therefore do not love God more than money, that we are indeed greedy? Is Jesus telling us that "treasure" is so deceitful, that the accumulation of it makes so much sense to our natural way of thinking—the light within us actually being darkness—that our evaluation of our adherence to His teachings and commandments can be quite wrong when we truly believe we are quite right?

Have we come to believe, because we are Christians, that of course, our eye is "good" and that our bodies are full of light, when, in reality, our eyes are "bad" and our bodies are full of darkness? Please, consider with me that this at least might be a possibility. Please consider that we have heaped riches to ourselves. We've done this, not because we're evil, but simply because we were born into and have inherited a church culture the basic assumptions of which we've accepted without questioning.

And that we've been deceived, because, as Jesus said, riches are deceiving.

So much of what we have done in the Church

concerning wealth and property makes sense to our way of thinking. The group grew larger, so we needed a larger space. The group grew larger, so we needed more people on staff to help the pastor care for them. We wanted our "house" to be accommodating, so we invested in sensible things so people would feel welcome. We wanted to attract seeking unbelievers, so we invested in furniture and media and music so they would feel welcome. Because the souls of those unbelievers are so precious, we invested in performance staff in order to attract them so they could hear the gospel.

It all makes sense. Unfortunately, it also made us rich, with a large appetite. That concerns me because we've placed ourselves in the position now of having the word that the Sower may speak to us choked out because of how much we've invested. It concerns me because it makes it very, very difficult to say yes to Jesus when and if He should say, "Sell all you possess and come follow Me." The solution? The answer isn't to get rid of all of our stuff. However, Jesus offers us this powerful challenge: "So therefore, any one of you who does not renounce all that he has cannot be my disciple" (Luke 14:33). If we want to be His disciples—if we pastors and leaders want to be His disciples—we must give up from our hearts all the financial investment we've made into our churches and be ready, at any moment, to sell all and give to the poor.

Are you willing, honestly and fervently, to do that?

If you are, then welcome to the ministry and the

discipleship of the most radical Being we'll ever have the privilege of knowing.

Chapter Five

What Is Leadership?

"A leader is one who, out of madness or goodness, volunteers to take upon himself the woe of the people. There are few men so foolish, hence the erratic quality of leadership in the world."
~John Updike

"The kings of the Gentiles exercise lordship over them, and those in authority over them are called benefactors. But not so with you. Rather, let the greatest among you become as the youngest, and the leader as one who serves."
~Jesus

Leadership has been the most taught and discussed topic in the American church in my lifetime. When I did a search recently on Amazon, there were 15,758 hits on the topic of Christian leadership. It makes sense. It doesn't take much reading in Scripture to find leadership being manifested in one form or another by the notable individuals in the Bible. Yet if we do a word search through the Scripture, we find a paucity of references under that word. Why is that? I think that the reason we find so little use of the word "leader" in Scripture is because that aspect, that virtue, is secondary in God's view. Perhaps not even secondary. Therefore, I'm troubled when we have made it our number one emphasis for so many years. If we read about God's leaders in Scripture, we'll find, overwhelmingly, an emphasis on only two traits: godliness and obedient, active faith in the power and ability of God.

Since thousands of books have been written on this topic, it would be foolhardy to attempt a comprehensive study in one chapter. However, if we look at what Moses, Joshua, Gideon and David did as leaders, we won't find much detail on *how* they did leadership. Over and over again, the recurring quality in these men is that they heard the words that God said, spoke them and acted upon them. The Lord powerfully did the rest.

> *If we read about God's leaders in Scripture, we'll find, overwhelmingly, an emphasis on only two traits: godliness and faith in the power and ability of God.*

It's that simple.
Simple, perhaps, but not easy.

Points of Departure 79

How did Moses lead? He heard the words of God and spoke them before the king of Egypt. God did the rest. Afterwards, Moses spoke, wrote down and acted upon what God articulated in his ear concerning His tabernacle and sacrificial system. Did some of these tasks require administration? Yes. However, is it administrative ability that Scripture acknowledges him for? Is Moses honored for the size of the group he led? Moses would have been the first to say that it wasn't he that led them, but God. We're told that he was a humble man. He stood up and spoke God's words to a very powerful sovereign. He interceded for Israel when they were disobedient and grumbling. Again, he did what the Lord told him to do, both in bringing God's people out of Egypt and leading them through the wilderness.

> *I am troubled by the possibility that Jesus would not be a leader in the Western Church today. Think with me here. What did Jesus do that has any resemblance to what our pastors and staffs do today?*

How did Joshua lead? What military strategy did he use to conquer Canaan? If possible, we could inquire of the people of Jericho to answer that question. Joshua did what God told him to do, and the Lord did the rest. It was an unlikely tactical approach.

The same question could be asked about Gideon. How did he lead the armies of Israel? Again, a highly unusual method of attack.

How did David lead? How, practically, did he supervise the kingdom of Israel? We know almost nothing about this. We do see him doing administrative and organizational tasks, such as in 1 Chronicles 23. However, it wasn't for how well he did these tasks that David was honored. He is revered in Scripture for being a man after God's heart. A courageous believer in God, a giant slayer. He was the sweet psalmist of Israel. And, yes, he was a repentant sinner. These are the qualities of David that the Bible emphasizes. How he led in a practical sense is barely noticeable.

How did Abraham lead? What did he do? He believed God, moved and acted in obedience to Him. God did the rest.

Were Isaiah, Jeremiah, Ezekiel—all the prophets—leaders? What did they do? They heard and spoke the words of God. He did the rest.

How leadership is done, in a practical manner, is almost totally ignored in Scripture, apart from hearing and doing what God says.

Let's take a look at Jesus, the almighty God, our Savior and Creator and upholder of all things. Was He a leader? I'm asking a serious question. I am troubled by the possibility that Jesus would not be a leader in the Western

Church today. Think with me here. What did Jesus do that has any resemblance to what our pastors and staffs do today? Again, seriously: What did Jesus actually do? He taught. He healed sick people and delivered those who were oppressed. He confronted the legalistic religious leadership of His day. He performed miracles. He died for our sins and rose to life. The only similarity between what He did and what we do is teaching, unless you're one of those in the minority who operate in the gifts of the Spirit.

How did Jesus organize His followers? As far as we can tell, there was almost no organization. He led and sent out seventy men, by twos (some manuscripts say seventy-two), and he ministered to twelve of them closely and three, intimately. How did He organize the seventy and the twelve? He told them, besides some instructions on what to take and what not take with them in certain instances, to "Heal the sick who are there and tell them, 'The kingdom of God is near you'" (Luke 10:9 NIV; 9:1-6). Can you imagine giving such a dearth of instruction to a group that we would send out today?

What did Jesus teach His disciples about leadership? We know the answer. He taught them to lead by being servants, by acting as if they were the youngest, not the oldest.

> The kings of the Gentiles exercise lordship over them, and those in authority over them are called benefactors. But not so

> with you. Rather, let the greatest among
> you become as the youngest, and the leader
> as one who serves (Luke 22:25-26).

Many of us know what it's like to be the youngest in the family, right? Or the newbie on the job? Age and experience have their advantages. However, Jesus teaches us that the greatest servant acts like the kid who just started shaving, who has no seniority. Is that how we lead today in the Western Church? Well, we say we do, by virtue of the fact that pastors and leaders give themselves sacrificially for the church and the staff, by teaching, counseling, working hard, building teams and programs and by remaining diligent. However, that isn't what Jesus meant when He talked about servant leadership. He was clear. Let's look at what He said in Matthew 20:25-28.

> You know that the rulers of the Gentiles
> lord it over them, and their great ones
> exercise authority over them. It shall not
> be so among you. But whoever would be
> great among you must be your servant, and
> whoever would be first among you must be
> your slave, even as the Son of Man came
> not to be served but to serve, and to give
> his life as a ransom for many.

What should catch our attention in this portion of

Jesus' teaching is that the Gentile rulers "exercise authority over them," but "it shall not be so among you."

It shall not be so among you. What am I, as a pastor or leader, to do with that? How could I possibly run a church without exercising authority over people? We run our churches as "the rulers of the Gentiles do." However, Jesus said, plainly, "It shall not be so among you." Why do we ignore Him in this?

But wait a minute. Didn't Jesus have authority? Of course He did. He had *spiritual* authority.

Was the authority Jesus had in the lives of the disciples effective? Again, it certainly didn't eliminate problems. None of Jesus' disciples seemed to get the full picture of His life and work while He was on earth. Judas betrayed Him, as Jesus knew He would. So here's a question: Why didn't Jesus, using His authority, "fire" Judas? Is the answer because Jesus knew Judas was necessary in order for all things to be fulfilled? Certainly. But let's look a little deeper. Jesus was willing to die in order for all things to be fulfilled, which means He was willing to have everything fall apart, at least temporarily. We don't think that way. We do all we can within our organizations to *keep* everything from falling apart. It's the nature of the system to do so. Look again with me at what Jesus said to His disciples about leadership. "… even as the Son of Man came not to be served but to serve, and to give his life as a ransom for many."

Not to be served, but to serve, to give his life. In Jesus' way of thinking, leading by serving included dying for others.

Jesus didn't have an organization to protect or an establishment the survival of which He had to insure in an earthly way. He had men. He had His Holy Spirit. Somehow, contrary to what we might think or do, He thought that this was sufficient. This is how He led.

May I say that again in another way? Jesus didn't seem to think it was paramount to have a defined, organized structure to leave behind after He ascended. Paramount? He didn't do that at all.

> *If our method of leadership is the one we should follow and adhere to, why didn't God Himself use it in the leadership ministry of Jesus?*

We do not follow Him. We lead, not as Jesus told us to, but as the "Gentiles" do.

What I'm going to ask next is a question we steadfastly ignore. If our method of leadership is the one we should follow and adhere to, why didn't God Himself use it in the leadership ministry of Jesus? Here is the second question we ignore. If our method of leadership is the one we should follow and adhere to, why didn't the early Church use it?

We should be brutally honest here. What we do is not biblical. Evangelical Christianity in the United States has, correctly and honorably, held to the Scripture as the inspired word of God, the very words of God Himself, written to us. Why, then, it must be asked, have we not followed Scripture in regard to how we lead the Church?

How about Paul? Did he have authority? Yes. Likewise, he had spiritual authority. He had this authority because of the miracles that had been performed through him and for having suffered for the Lord and His Church, which he points out in his apostolic defense. He also laid claim to having spiritual power.

But did Paul have the kind of authority that pastors and leaders wield in the Church today? How did Paul exercise authority in the early Church? Ecclesiastical power? He said this interesting thing in 1 Corinthians 4:19-20: "But I will come to you soon, if the Lord wills, and I will find out not the talk of these arrogant people but their power. For the kingdom of God does not consist in talk but in power." What kind of power was Paul referring to? Ecclesiastical power? No. What Paul wielded was spiritual power.

Was that spiritual leadership effective? Again, there clearly were problems. It didn't take much time before there was divisiveness in Corinth and death-producing legalism at Galatia. Paul exhorted and attempted to persuade the believers in these places to correct these issues. However, what authoritative structure did he build? He told Timothy to appoint elders in every church, listing for him the qualities needed (1Timothy 3:2-12). What other organizational things did Paul set up or establish? I can find none.

****

I don't find leader or leadership in the list of ministries in Ephesians 4:11-14:

> And he gave the apostles, the prophets, the evangelists, the pastors and teachers, to equip the saints for the work of ministry, for building up the body of Christ, until we all attain to the unity of the faith and of the knowledge of the Son of God, to mature manhood, to the measure of the stature of the fullness of Christ, so that we may no longer be children, tossed to and fro by the waves and carried about by every wind of doctrine, by human cunning, by craftiness in deceitful schemes.

Nor do I see it in 1 Corinthians 12:27-28:

> Now you are the body of Christ and individually members of it. And God has appointed in the church first apostles, second prophets, third teachers, then miracles, then gifts of healing, helping, administrating, and various kinds of tongues.

In fact, some of what we call leadership is administrating, and while it is needful, it's at the bottom of the list, just above tongues.

I do, however, finally find it toward the bottom of the list of gifts in Romans 12:4-8:

> For as in one body we have many members, and the members do not all have the same function, so we, though many, are one body in Christ, and individually members one of another. Having gifts that differ according to the grace given to us, let us use them: if prophecy, in proportion to our faith; if service, in our serving; the one who teaches, in his teaching; the one who exhorts, in his exhortation; the one who contributes, in generosity; the one who leads, with zeal; the one who does acts of mercy, with cheerfulness.

That Paul either ignored the ministry of leadership or put it almost dead last in the Romans 12 gift inventory gives me pause. Paul is indicating that the gift of leadership should not be exalted—it should be minimized. This makes perfect sense, in light of our knowledge of human nature and what the disciples were concerned about when they were walking with their Master: "A dispute also arose among them, as to which of them was to be regarded as the greatest" (Luke 22:24).

In contrast, what do we find at the top of these lists? Prophecy is consistently first or second. Paul says in 1 Corinthians 14:1, "Pursue love, and earnestly desire the spiritual gifts, especially that you may prophesy." He repeats this admonition at the end of the chapter. "So, my brothers, earnestly desire to prophesy..." (vs. 39a). Paul tells us to earnestly desire the spiritual gifts—earnestly. Twice, he tells us to desire to prophesy. Where is leadership in all this? Why doesn't he say, "Earnestly desire to lead?" Is it because doing these things actually *is* leading? Love is also high in importance in Paul's view and is considered the greatest ministry of all, certainly required if one is to "lead," which, according to Jesus, looks much like being a slave.

Paul lists the gifts in 1 Corinthians 12:4-11, but wisdom, knowledge and faith are prominent in these verses.

> *Paul tells us to earnestly desire the spiritual gifts—earnestly. Twice, he tells us to desire to prophesy. Where is leadership in all this? Why doesn't he say, "Earnestly desire to lead?"*

> Now there are varieties of gifts, but the same Spirit; and there are varieties of service, but the same Lord; and there are varieties of activities, but it is the same God who empowers them all in everyone. To each is given the manifestation of the Spirit for the common good. To one is given through the Spirit the utterance of wisdom, and to another the utterance of knowledge according to the same Spirit, to another faith by the same Spirit, to another gifts of healing by the one Spirit, to another the working of miracles, to another prophecy, to another the ability to distinguish between spirits, to another various kinds of tongues, to another the interpretation of tongues. All these are empowered by one and the same Spirit, who apportions to each one individually as he wills.

Do you see the gift of leadership here?

There are a couple of places where the idea of being over someone or ruling them is in the New Testament. One is in 1 Timothy 5:17: "Let the elders who rule well be considered worthy of double honor, especially those who labor in preaching and teaching." The other is in 1 Thessalonians 5:12-13. "We ask you, brothers, to respect those who labor among you and are over you in the Lord and admonish you, and to esteem them very highly in love because of their work. Be at peace among yourselves."

> *We don't work hard to operate in the supernatural power of God, as every leader in the Bible did—because we're too hard at work building and organizing a religious structure.*

However, in light of what Jesus taught about leadership, I must ask what "rule well" and "over you in the Lord" mean here. If Jesus meant what He said, "leading" would not be "ruling as the Gentiles do," but being a slave to the members of our group, while having spiritual authority. The way we would "lead" as Peter, the one who walked with Jesus, instructed:

> ...shepherd the flock of God that is among you, exercising oversight, not under compulsion, but willingly, as God would have you; not for shameful gain, but eagerly; not domineering over those in your charge, but being examples to the flock (1 Peter 5:2-3).

Exercise oversight and lead by example, Peter tells us, not with ecclesiastical or organizational authority.

My opinion is that we have organized our churches, established programs and built teams in ways that neither Jesus, the Lord of the Church, nor the leaders of the early Church did. My opinion is that this method of leadership has played very well into our Western view of hard work, individualism and materialism. We lead, as Jesus instructed us not to, as the Gentiles do. We work hard, there is no doubt about that, but we work hard to build an organization that is contrary to the biblical pattern. We don't work hard to simply, purely follow Jesus, hear God's words and act upon them, while eschewing Gentile leadership principles, according to the biblical pattern. We don't work hard to operate in the supernatural power of God, as every leader in the Bible did—because we're too hard at work building and organizing a religious structure.

So the question: Is it possible for us, in today's Western Church, to lead biblically?

Chapter Six

What Is Suffering?

"God had one son on earth without sin, but never one without suffering."
~Saint Augustine

"It wasn't until we got over the self pity that we were able to accept suffering as a part of our life with Christ. A man or woman reaches this plane only when he or she ceases to be the hero."
~Corazon Aquino

We are wired, physically and mentally, to avoid suffering. Nobody enjoys affliction, at least certainly no one I know. Understandably, we would rather live in comfort and with a minimum of pain during our brief sojourn on the earth. However, many people deny this human preference to avoid affliction and choose to willingly suffer in service to others, to their country or to God. In most cases, we honor those who travel this road.

Jesus Himself suffered, not for Himself, but for others, for the inhabitants of this dark, rebellious planet. It shouldn't surprise us, then, since He calls us to follow Him, that He expects us to do the same. Jesus has offered up some extremely challenging statements concerning suffering and sacrifice. Twice in Matthew, He exhorted those who would follow Him to be willing to die—not just die, but die a humiliating, excruciatingly painful death.

> And whoever does not take his cross and follow me is not worthy of me. Whoever finds his life will lose it, and whoever loses his life for my sake will find it (Matthew 10:38-39).

Not worthy, He says. We are not worthy of Jesus unless we are willing to die for Him. This is stunning. We might be believers. We might be church attendees. We might be really nice people. But we will not be worthy of Him unless we make the choice, in our hearts, to offer our lives in sacrifice to Him.

> *We are not worthy of Jesus unless we are willing to die for Him. This is stunning*

"Then Jesus told his disciples, 'If anyone would come

after me, let him deny himself and take up his cross and follow me'" (Matthew 16:24).

There is only one way to follow Jesus: self-denial to the point of death.

In Luke, Jesus uses the cross to challenge the nature and quality of our discipleship: "Whoever does not bear his own cross and come after me cannot be my disciple" (Luke 14:27).

Let's allow those words to sink down into our ears. This is a qualification for discipleship. We cannot be a disciple of Jesus unless we are willing to choose, literally, to die.

Those who were listening had no illusions about what Jesus said. In their homeland, they saw criminals and revolutionaries crucified on Roman crosses all the time. Let's bring this home. You and I are sitting in a coffee shop, enjoying a hot drink and great conversation. Jesus walks in through the door and says, "There is a crowd of people outside the door who, if you walk outside with Me right now, are going to beat you senseless with crowbars and metal pipes. If you do this, you'll be saving the life of Li Linbin, a forty-year-old former barber and alcoholic who lives on the streets in Guangzhou, as well as his family. But you can choose. You can choose to walk out the door or choose not to. You can stay here and drink your coffee, if you wish. It's your decision."

Which would you choose? I know what my answer is, and I'm not particularly happy with it. I would choose to continue to sip my double-tall, peppermint mocha, thank you very much.

The choice I seem to be unwilling to make is the same choice that Jesus willingly made. We often tell people that if they were the only person on earth, Jesus would have died for them. Yet, in the hypothetical scenario presented above, I realized that I wasn't willing to die for some unknown, insignificant man and his family in China. I see, reluctantly, how far I am from the heart of Jesus. However, Peter tells us to arm ourselves with the same way of thinking that Jesus had:

> Since therefore Christ suffered in the flesh, arm yourselves with the same way of thinking, for whoever has suffered in the flesh has ceased from sin, so as to live for the rest of the time in the flesh no longer for human passions but for the will of God (1 Peter 4:1-2).

There is only one way that I will ever be willing to say yes to His sacrificial question, and that is to pray for a heart that is willing to do such a thing. I do not have that heart.

I must ask for it.

The recognition of the call to suffering in the lives of followers of Jesus continues in the writings of Paul and Peter. In Acts 14:21-22, Luke writes about what Paul preached in Lystra, Iconium and Antioch:

> They preached the good news in that city and won a large number of disciples. Then they returned to Lystra, Iconium and Antioch, strengthening the disciples and encouraging them to remain true to the faith. "We must go through many hardships to enter the kingdom of God," they said (NIV).

That last sentence is an interesting statement, isn't it? We must go through many hardships to enter the kingdom of God. Rulership with God, apparently, has to do with the sacrificial self-denial that comes through experiencing hardship, as well as knowing Jesus, not with the accumulation of knowledge or with any kind of power. This makes sense. "Blessed are the poor in spirit," Jesus said, "for theirs is the kingdom of God." Recognizing and admitting how poor we are without God helps us enter the kingdom, the place where God rules. If we think we're rich in and by ourselves, well, we have our riches—but we will not be rich in God. This "poverty of spirit" requires ongoing requests to God from our hearts and in prayer, that God would in fact make us poor in spirit, because the human tendency is exactly the opposite—to be rich in and by ourselves.

So, according to Scripture, there is a relationship between being poor in spirit and entering God's kingdom. And we know, don't we, that one of the ways God uses to show us how weak and needy we are, how desperately we need Him, is through trouble and trial. This is why it makes sense when Peter seems to make a connection with salvation itself and suffering trials.

> In this you rejoice, though now for a little while, if necessary, you have been grieved by various trials, so that the tested genuineness of your faith—more precious than gold that perishes though it is tested by fire—may be found to result in praise and glory and honor at the revelation of Jesus Christ. Though you have not seen him, you love him. Though you do not now see him, you believe in him and rejoice with joy that is inexpressible and filled with glory, obtaining the outcome of your faith, the salvation of your souls" (1 Peter 1:6-9).

Peter tells us that the suffering we endure will test the genuineness of our faith and, that if our faith does prove to be genuine, it will bring glory to the Lord Jesus. These trials that we experience, Peter says, will benefit in obtaining the outcome of that faith: the salvation of our souls.

Peter also tells us that we have been called to suffer in order to follow Jesus.

> For what credit is it if, when you sin and are beaten for it, you endure? But if when you do good and suffer for it you endure, this is a gracious thing in the sight of God. *For to this you have been called, because Christ also suffered for you, leaving you an example, so that you might follow in his steps* (1 Peter 2:20-21, emphasis mine).

And then in the same letter, Peter writes that we should prepare ourselves to suffer, to arm ourselves with the same attitude Jesus had.

> So then, since Christ suffered physical pain, you must arm yourselves with the same attitude he had, and be ready to suffer, too. For if you have suffered physically for Christ, you have finished with sin. You won't spend the rest of your lives chasing your own desires, but you will be anxious to do the will of God (1 Peter 4:1-2 NLT).

This is why I think Paul actually *desired* that he might suffer like Jesus. "…that I may know him and the power of his resurrection, and may share his sufferings, becoming like him in his death, that by any means possible I may attain the resurrection from the dead" (Philippians 3:10-11). There is some disagreement about whether Paul meant walking in the power of resurrection during his lifetime or physical resurrection at his death; however, wherever our exegesis leads us, one thing is clear: as far as Paul was concerned, sharing in the sufferings of Jesus and becoming like Him in His death was linked with sharing in that resurrection.

> We in the West rarely have to deal with physical suffering as a result of our testimony concerning Jesus Christ. We don't have to give up our lives the way many do in the world today. But we must be willing to do so.

We in the West rarely have to deal with physical suffering as a result of our testimony concerning Jesus Christ. We don't have to give up our lives the way many do in the world today.

But we must be willing to do so.

****

If you're like me, you've heard more than once that we are joint heirs with Christ. We are God's very own children! True enough. However, let's look more closely at what Paul said.

> The Spirit himself bears witness with our spirit that we are children of God, and if children, then heirs—heirs of God and fellow heirs with Christ, provided we suffer with him in order that we may also be glorified with him (Romans 8:16-17).

How often have you heard from a teacher that our inheritance in Christ might be dependent upon our suffering? What are we going to do with this? Are we to tell our people that they must suffer if they're going to share in their inheritance in Christ?

And what should we pastors do with this knowledge?

Consider this from Paul, which he wrote to Timothy:

> Therefore do not be ashamed of the testimony about our Lord, nor of me his prisoner, but share in suffering for the gospel by the power of God, who saved us and called us to a holy calling, not because of our works but because of his

own purpose and grace, which he gave us in Christ Jesus before the ages began, and which now has been manifested through the appearing of our Savior Christ Jesus, who abolished death and brought life and immortality to light through the gospel, for which I was appointed a preacher and apostle and teacher, which is why I suffer as I do (2 Timothy 1:8-12a).

Is this a command? Or is this meant only for Timothy? We've already seen, however, in Romans 8:17, that our inheritance seems, somehow, to be associated with suffering: "... heirs of God and fellow heirs with Christ, provided we suffer with him in order that we may also be glorified with him."

> *However, shouldn't we take a careful look at how we diligently strive to avoid suffering loss? And how we strive to avoid it in the structures where we minister, the local church?*

Paul wrote much the same to the church at Philippi: "For it has been granted to you that for the sake of Christ you should not only believe in him but also suffer for his sake, engaged in the same conflict that you saw I had and now hear that I still have" (Philippians 1:29-30). "It has been granted to you...that you should...suffer for his sake..." Strong's Lexicon defines "granted" here as "to do something pleasant or agreeable (to one), to do a favor to, gratify."

How important was suffering for the sake of Christ to Paul? He desired it because he believed that it would bring gain in his spiritual life. I refer again to that portion in Philippians 3:10-11, where he writes "...that I may know him and the power of his resurrection, and may share his sufferings, becoming like him in his death, that by any means possible I may attain the resurrection from the dead."

I'm not advocating beating ourselves with a stick so we can be more pious Christians. That's not piety; that's stupidity. However, shouldn't we take a careful look at how we diligently strive to avoid suffering loss? And how we strive to avoid it in the structures where we minister, the local church?

****

What does this call to suffering mean for the institution we call the Church? Clearly, biblically, the followers of Jesus Christ who are within this institution are called to suffer. But what about the institution itself? There may be extraordinarily challenging times for this organization if we take seriously this radical call to follow Jesus and deny ourselves. We may be made poor. We may endure difficult times. We may suffer loss and be diminished.

And we know that sometimes our churches are diminished. Numbers fall off. Volunteerism lags. Sometimes our churches are made poor. What, typically, is our response when such things begin to happen?

Of course, we pray, as we should. We ask for more money. We ask for more volunteers. And we do it in a way that isn't dishonest, certainly, but we—let's be transparent here—do it in a way that won't appear negative to the hearers. "Never beg." "Never appear desperate." "Always be upbeat in your presentation." I mean, after all, who wants to give money to help support a sinking ship? Believe me—I've been in those staff meetings—I know.

We tread precariously close to fulfilling this axiom from corporate America: Image is everything.

But biblically, isn't suffering loss a good thing? Doesn't it bring us, when we realize how poor we are in spirit, to a place of rulership, into God's kingdom, as Jesus taught? Don't trials make us perfect and complete?

> Count it all joy, my brothers, when you meet trials of various kinds, for you know that the testing of your faith produces steadfastness. And let steadfastness have its full effect, that you may be perfect and complete, lacking in nothing
> (James 1:2-4).

Why do we attempt to hide it? Is it because we're more concerned about the numerical growth of the local institution than we are about our Christlikeness? We honor individual Christians who suffer. We have compassion on them. Why is it different for this institution we call the local church?

> *What Scripture values is sacrificial dedication to Jesus Christ. What the evangelical church today values is numerical growth.*

It's different because the way we view the Church today is at odds with the biblical view of what has value and what is honorable. What Scripture values is sacrificial dedication to Jesus Christ. What the evangelical church today values is numerical growth.

Maybe, just maybe, God is calling this local institution—your church—to suffer or to experience loss. I do not hope this would be the case. My fervent desire is that your church would effectively reach people for Jesus and make disciples, as Jesus told us to, and never have to suffer at all. However, shouldn't we carefully consider the way Jesus said spiritual fruit is created? He said, "Truly, truly, I say to you, unless a grain of wheat falls into the earth and dies, it remains alone; but if it dies, it bears much fruit" (John 12:24). Perhaps, just perhaps, Jesus is calling us on the commitment we made to Him, to give our lives to Him, which included denying ourselves and the things to which we attach ourselves. Is it possible for us to entertain the possibility that the Lord would want us to deny ourselves, concerning our churches? Wouldn't it be a good, spiritual place to be, to open our hands and "die" to the life or "success" of our church?

If we can't entertain that possibility, why can't we?

We in the Western Church live in a place where the existence of our local institution has taken precedence over our vital, life-denying life in Jesus Christ. Nothing is more important, from our point of view, than the existence, the thriving, of our church. Nothing. Not even bringing forth fruit in Jesus.

"But our church should—it must—continue to exist!" you may say. "Look at all the people who are coming to Christ! Look at all the people who are being encouraged to live a godly lifestyle!"

I don't doubt it.

Then again, I do doubt that people would stop coming to Christ or living a godly lifestyle if your particular church were to be diminished numerically.

The Jewish people were convinced, because of God's promise, that there would always be a ruler on David's throne, that there was no way that Jerusalem could ever be captured by a foreign power or destroyed. However, as we know, it was conquered, more than once. Do our attitudes about our churches sound a bit like the inhabitants of Jerusalem and the priests when they were told by the prophets that the city and the temple would be destroyed? "Impossible! This is God's throne! He's made promises to Israel!"

How do we go about this? How do we voluntarily suffer? Admittedly, some of the suffering Paul refers to is because Christians were being persecuted by the Roman government and the Jewish religious system for following Jesus and for preaching the gospel. Even though the United States and Europe are post-Christian societies, we have not yet entered into the level of persecution that Paul and the early disciples did, and that many throughout the world since then have and even now, do. However, it seems clear that we should, somehow, intentionally prepare ourselves to suffer. Again, Peter wrote:

> Since therefore Christ suffered in the flesh, arm yourselves with the same way of thinking, for whoever has suffered in the flesh has ceased from sin, so as to live for the rest of the time in the flesh no longer for human passions but for the will of God (1 Peter 4:1-2).

Arm yourselves with the same way of thinking, Peter says, since Christ suffered in the flesh. There is a martial sense to this expression "arm yourselves" in the Greek, and that would seem to be necessary. In order to take on the same mind, the same way of thinking—to suffer in the flesh—we would need to strongly prepare ourselves, like soldiers do, because our own way of thinking as well as the thinking of the world would vigorously militate against this stance, because we love comfort.

Well, I do, anyway. And it makes me a bit nervous that Paul lists the following trait among others that will characterize those who live in the last days: They will be "...lovers of pleasure rather than lovers of God..." (2 Timothy 3:4b).

> *It is not in our makeup to want to choose suffering over pleasure. We will have to ask for a change of heart.*

How should we respond to these admonitions to suffer? This is a difficult question. Perhaps we can find some guidance in the words of John:

> And this is the confidence that we have toward him, that if we ask anything according to his will he hears us. And if we know that he hears us in whatever we ask, we know that we have the requests that we have asked of him (1 John 5:14-15).

Since we are told that we have been called to suffer because Christ suffered for us, we know it is His will.

However, we do not naturally have this desire to deny ourselves in this way. It is not in our makeup to want to choose suffering over pleasure.

We will have to ask for a change of heart.

How do we reconcile this call to suffer with this contemporary statement: "A healthy church is a growing church"? The Church in the New Testament grew in spite of persecution and suffering. Perhaps one of the reasons for that growth was their obedience to Jesus when He said, "If anyone would come after me, let him deny himself and take up his cross and follow me" (Mark 8:34b). The followership of those early disciples, a bright, burning light, inspired others to become Christians. We do not offer the world such a challenging example. We are unwilling to die. So perhaps we should say, "A healthy church is one that is willing to die."

Certainly a biblical church is.

Chapter Seven

What Is Strong?

*"When you come together, each one has a hymn,
a lesson, a revelation, a tongue, or an interpretation.
Let all things be done for building up."*
~Paul, the apostle

Here's a tip about how to make your pastor roll his eyes when he's closed the door to his office after a conversation with you: Tell him that you're no longer being fed at his church. Why would your pastor roll his eyes? Because he doesn't believe that it's solely his responsibility to feed you and doesn't understand why you don't get that. He thinks that it's *your* responsibility to have a deep, dynamic relationship with the Lord, which focuses primarily on Bible study and a personal prayer life.

And he's right.

But only partly right.

Pastors shouldn't be surprised that this complaint reoccurs in their churches, and it's not just because people don't get it, that they are the ones who are responsible for feeding themselves. The way we in the Church currently do things, and the very structure that we're immersed in, *works against* believers doing what we want them to do in order to be strong believers.

We've made them co-dependent.

We, the leadership, have become the enablers of weak Christians. We've created, by virtue of our values and resulting structure, generations of believers who consider themselves members of a local body—most of them, anyway—primarily in order to have their needs met. Again, that shouldn't surprise us. They come into our churches, and we offer them free coffee and beverages. They take their kids to our children's ministries, where we offer free childcare and classes that teach young people about being Christians. After they enter the auditorium and sit in the comfortable chairs we've provided, we lead them into worship, having selected the songs for them that will help them praise God. We choose the style in which they worship. They listen to us as we teach, after we have done the work of hermeneutics, exegesis and study for them. We flash the scripture verses up on the screen for them, in case they didn't bring their Bibles. We provide these services because we want those who attend our churches to feel welcome and provided for, and so they will come back and bring their friends with them. We work diligently at these tasks so we can do evangelism at our services, because we don't want unbelievers to have to leap over a church-induced, religious cultural gap. It all makes sense.

However we have, by the virtue of our ministries, with the best of intentions, created Christian adherents whose foundational experiences in the Church are centered around "I."

> *The way we in the Church currently do things, and the very structure that we're immersed in, works against believers doing what we want them to do in order to be strong believers. We've made them co-dependent.*

I'm not being fed here.

I don't like the worship.

I don't like the pastor.

I like the pastor. He's a great teacher, but I don't want to come unless he's speaking. Pastor Mark is okay, but…

I don't like the teaching.

I don't like the childcare.

I don't like the situation with the parking.

I don't like it because it's too big.

I don't like it because it's too small.

I.

We attempt to get people involved by teaching about

the value of participation and offering opportunities to serve. We have developed programs to reach out to the community. We sign up parents, grandparents and teenagers to serve in kids' programs and nurseries. We organize mission trips abroad. Certainly, there is nothing about any one of these programs that is misguided in and of itself. But none of them addresses the "I"-centered culture we have created or causes people to take responsibility, in a biblical way, for their own spiritual growth or for that of other believers, during our meetings. They're simply serving in church programs. Gathering together without requiring individual responsibility for one's own spiritual maturity and the strengthening of others won't encourage Christian growth—it encourages Christian parasitism.

Does the Bible indicate what kind of church meeting will build up believers? Yes. Paul tells us.

> What then, brothers? When you come together, each one has a hymn, a lesson, a revelation, a tongue, or an interpretation. Let all things be done for building up (1 Corinthians 14:26).

When I go to church, according to this verse, it is my responsibility to bring a hymn, a lesson, a revelation; something that God has shown me earlier or that He is doing right then, supernaturally, by His Spirit. However, as much emphasis as we've placed on meeting in small groups and Bible studies, those admittedly more intimate formats in and of themselves don't require this of us. In a small group structure, we still have one person teaching. Individuals might contribute to the prayer time or to

> *Gathering together without requiring individual responsibility for one's own spiritual maturity and the strengthening of others won't encourage Christian growth—it encourages Christian parasitism.*

the discussion, but more than likely they're not coming prepared to input something from the Bible that they have studied on our own. It's rare that they'll be given an opportunity to bring a song or to be involved with the supernatural gifts that 1 Corinthians 14:26 mentions. Small groups, although more intimate, are closer to "Honey, I shrunk the church," than they are to the biblical model.

1 Corinthians 14:26, a scripture that describes a biblical church meeting, has very little meaning for us in the contemporary church. This is stunning. It's stunning because it is in the Bible, and we ignore it.

I once had a conversation with an associate pastor at the last church at which I was employed. This man was a father with two young children and was the pastor of discipleship. He was leading a small group, and I asked him how it was going.

"Awesome!" he replied.

"What are you doing?" I asked. I wondered what it would take to have an awesome small group.

"We're playing video games. It's awesome."

Doing church as the early Church did, just using the small gathering structure that they used, is only part of the biblical answer. If we want strong, "self-fed" believers, we must follow what Paul describes in 1 Corinthians 14:26 as well as the example in Acts 2:42: breaking bread, sharing the apostles' teaching and praying. In this biblical model, each member has responsibility to bring something to edify others. However, it will be a struggle. We have become so toxified by the way we do church, so used to being passive listeners, so accustomed

> We have become so toxified by the way we do church, so used to being passive listeners, so accustomed to having someone else take the responsibility for the edification of our fellow believers, that it will take a strong, intentional effort to move past it, to be detoxified.

to having someone else take the responsibility for the edification of our fellow believers, that it will take a strong, intentional effort to move past it, to be *de*toxified.

Because we've taken away this requirement to be responsible and prepared to bring something to our gatherings, or to speak something God may have said to us before the meeting or when it's in progress, too many believers are selfish and immature when it comes to life in the Church. We've created passive churchgoers. Church attendees come to our buildings, sing along with our worship teams, say hello and talk about relatively insignificant issues during the short time they have to interact with each other, and then they go home. What are their spiritual lives like? We'll probably never know. Are they being used by God to edify other believers in love, with biblical gifts of the Spirit? Again, we'll probably never know.

****

Sometimes we hear pastors and leaders talk about how too many people are still spiritual babies and need milk, because they don't have a prayer or devotional life or don't go to church in a committed way. Biblically, needing milk has nothing to do with these things. The writer of Hebrews told his readers that they needed milk because they had become "dull of hearing." Apparently, though they had been Christians for some time, they were "unskilled in the word of righteousness" and needed someone to teach them "the basic principles of the oracles of God." Then he says, "But solid food is for the mature, for those who have their powers of discernment trained by constant practice to distinguish good from evil" (Hebrews 5:11-14). How were they to have that "constant practice" so they could have their powers of discernment trained? It was either going to happen out in the marketplace or when they gathered, not in their private, devotional lives.

In his first letter to the Corinthians, Paul said,

> But I, brothers, could not address you as spiritual people, but as people of the flesh, as infants in Christ. I fed you with milk, not solid food, for you were not ready for it. And even now you are not yet ready, for you are still of the flesh. For while there is jealousy and strife among you, are you not of the flesh and behaving only in a human way? For when one says, "I follow Paul," and another, "I follow Apollos," are you not being merely human?
> (1 Corinthians 3:1-4).

Paul told the Corinthians that the reason they were infants was because they were following one particular man and not another, not because they had insufficient devotional lives. However, following a particular man is exactly the place where we have put our people. We have, for the bulk of our teaching times, one person who teaches while others fill in when he is absent. Our church attendance is all too often built around one dynamic individual. Because we've created consumer Christians, attendance will drop when this person, probably the senior pastor, isn't up front teaching. We'll change churches if a new pastor is installed because "we don't like his teaching." Some say they follow Pastor Mike. Others say they follow Pastor Bill. Therefore, according to Paul, our members are "people of the flesh" and "infants in Christ."

This is the system in which we live and breathe in our Christian church tradition. We don't know of any other. However we should, because there is another way, and it's the only way Scripture indicates how to conduct church. Unfortunately, the way that is revealed to us is so difficult and contrary to our Western conventions that we can't accept it. In fact, implementing a structure for church that the Bible itself demonstrates seems unthinkable, impossible to us. If our church experience was to conform to this biblical pattern, it would largely disestablish what church has come to mean for us. We can't imagine that this is necessary, even though it's plain in Scripture. Thus, we continue, by our tradition, to have some who are strong—mostly paid and volunteer staff, while the majority is weak.

Biblically, what does make us strong?

Obviously, the Lord:
The scriptural examples are too numerous to list, but here is one: "And after you have suffered a little while, the God of all grace, who has called you to his eternal glory in Christ, will himself restore, confirm, strengthen, and establish you"
(1 Peter 5:10).

Prayer:
"But you, beloved, build yourselves up in your most holy faith; pray in the Holy Spirit; keep yourselves in the love of God, waiting for the mercy of our Lord Jesus Christ that leads to eternal life"
(Jude 20-21). See also Matthew 26:41, James 5:13 and Luke 22:32.

Being weak:
"For when I am weak, then I am strong"
(2 Corinthians 12:10b).

Sharing our faith with each other:
"For I long to see you, that I may impart to you some spiritual gift to strengthen you—that is, that we may be mutually encouraged by each other's faith, both yours and mine" (Romans 1:11-12).

Grace:
"You then, my child, be strengthened by the grace that is in Christ Jesus..."   (2 Timothy 2:1).

The gifts of the Spirit, ministered through believers:
"So with yourselves, since you are eager for manifestations of the Spirit, strive to excel in building up the church"   (1 Corinthians 14:12).

The ministry of apostles, prophets, evangelists, shepherds and teachers:
"And he gave the apostles, the prophets, the evangelists, the pastors and teachers, to equip the saints for the work of ministry, for building up the body of Christ..." (Ephesians 4:11-12).

Love:
"Now concerning food offered to idols: we know that 'all of us possess knowledge.' This 'knowledge' puffs up, but love builds up" (1 Corinthians 8:1).

Speaking in tongues and prophesying:
"The one who speaks in a tongue builds up himself, but the one who prophesies builds up the church" (1 Corinthians 14:4).

Clearly, when the New Testament talks about making believers strong, its focus is not only on one's individual prayer life but also on the ministry of the Church, whether it's ministering in love or by means of the gifts and manifestations of the Spirit. It makes sense, then, given this emphasis on the strengthening that the Church provides, that Paul would teach that divisions in the Church—saying we're followers of one person and not another—would cause us to be as weak as infants. If we're concerned about which men or women are ministering to us, the focal point of our church life is more about us—what is strengthening to us, only—rather than what we can bring that builds up other believers. Our focus is...out of focus. It is on us.

In our highly individualized Western Church, we have emphasized one's personal devotional life as the source of our strength. Now, in no way do I want to diminish the importance of a strong life of prayer and knowledge of God's word. Both are vital in our Christian lives. But we have weakened the flock because we have created a consumer-oriented, passive Church, a Church that desperately needs the strengthening that each member offers, but that has denied the biblical model with which that can be accomplished.

Is it easy to implement this biblical model? Most certainly not. It is much less demanding, from an earthly point of view, to have five minute exchanges—as sincere as they are—in the foyer or fellowship hall. It is easier to meet together once a week in small groups to study the

Bible or a recently released book on a contemporary topic than to have spent time before the gathering, preparing and studying. It is more difficult to wait on the Lord than to stick to an established agenda. I'm not advocating discontinuing such small group activities. I'm advocating providing a structure that allows for the model we see in 1 Corinthians 14:26 and Acts 2:42. In our present context, we learn. We study Scripture. We fellowship. But we do not take individual responsibility to bring something to a gathering that is meant to strengthen believers or to seek God during the meeting with the same goal in mind. We do not have a format that allows for the gifts of the Holy Spirit to operate with the aim of building up believers. We don't hear prophecies in a small group context where such oracles can be judged, as the Bible instructs us.

What is perplexing about our current structure is that prophecy has been relegated to a place of almost complete insignificance in the majority of our churches, while, in amazing contrast, it is the first or second gift listed in all three of the gift and ministry lists in Ephesians 4:11-14, 1 Corinthians 12:27-28 and Romans 12:4-8.

Prophecy is huge is Scripture. Enormous. It seems incredible that I should have to mention this. We know that Moses was a prophet, as were Samuel and David, and, obviously, so were all the great prophets after whom books of the Bible are named. Jesus was a prophet, and we see prophets functioning in the Book of Acts. Prophets are honored in Scripture. What has happened? Is prophecy ignored because it is messy, because people might get it wrong or because there will be people speaking who have impure motivations? Yes. It is messy. The prophet Jeremiah addressed many condemnations to false prophets. However, he was a prophet himself. Those disobedient men didn't invalidate his ministry.

Yes, it can be awkward, but Paul clearly taught how to deal with this. In 1 Corinthians 14:29, he said, "Let two or three prophets speak, and let the others weigh what is said." He also said, "Do not despise prophecies, but test everything; hold fast what is good" (1 Thessalonians 5:20-21). Why would Paul instruct us not to despise prophesies? We can't be sure, but we could assume it was for the same reasons we tend to "despise" them today. Sometimes they don't pass the Scriptural test. In other instances, they seem silly, even comical, and we wonder what the real source or motivation of the utterance is. Regardless of how untidy prophecies are, that they are biblical is beyond dispute. We deny their operation to our detriment.

> ..., *the functioning of prophecy—so prevalent in Scripture—isn't even on the radar in most of our churches.*

However, the functioning of prophecy—so prevalent in Scripture—isn't even on the radar in most of our churches.

It's difficult to follow this scriptural example today because of the nature of the structure of our meetings. Even if we do allow for prophecy in our meetings, there is no vehicle for "others to weigh what is said." We do not give an opportunity for, as the writer of Hebrews said, their powers of discernment to be "trained by constant practice to distinguish good from evil" (Hebrews 5:14b).

This rebuke to Israel from the prophet Amos gives me pause, as I consider the current condition of the Western Church: "But you made the Nazirites drink wine, and commanded the prophets, saying, 'You shall not prophesy'" (Amos 2:12). When Amos was a prophet, Israel had turned its back on God, had fallen away from Him. What Amos mentions about forbidding prophesy was part of that rejection. What does that say about us, that we also have forbidden prophesy?

Consider what the prophet Hosea said in these words of rebuke to Israel, which had fallen away from God: "The prophet is a fool; the man of the spirit is mad, because of your great iniquity and great hatred" (Hosea 9:7b).

Perhaps we should bear the weight of responsibility if we perceive our prophets to be fools and people of the Spirit as mad. Something has gone really wrong in the Church.

This is tragic. In no way am I saying that our people and our leaders aren't hearing from God. I'm sure they are. However, the absence of the momentously significant ministry and use in our meetings of the prophet, given its importance in Scripture, is distressing. It's even more distressing that we don't even care—or are even aware—that it's absent. Again, when we lay what we do in our gatherings alongside what the Bible indicates is normal church life, we are missing the mark in an appalling way.

What are we to do? What will it take to get us to a biblical standard of how church is done? It will take a radical commitment to the truth of the word of God. What will that look like? I cannot say what that will be for individual churches. My goal is not to lay out a ten-point strategy for biblical, ecclesiastical behavior. My goal is to challenge us to adhere to Scripture and to ask God how to get there.

And, by His grace, He will.

Afterword

I trust that what you have read in the preceding pages has challenged you. It is my earnest hope and my prayer that the Holy Spirit has been at work as you have considered the biblical values for the Church that I've attempted to present here. Otherwise, these are just spots of ink on quickly decaying paper.

I am not angry at the Church, nor am I bitter. I will admit to cynicism, but hopefully any arrogance or legalism that sprang forth in me when I began this exigent comparison of biblical values to those in the contemporary evangelical church has been replaced by compassionate concern and intercession. The Church is the representation of Jesus on the earth. She needs to be—indeed, she will be—His obedient bride, bringing His life and light to this dark and rebellious planet. No, the genesis for this study was not disenchantment with the Church. It originated from what the Lord has been doing in my life the last few years: a drawing to pursue a deeper, more intimate relationship with Him. This invitation to intimacy has been profoundly life-changing and challenging because our Savior is the most amazing Being imaginable. He is stunningly creative. Powerful beyond our comprehension. So massive in His intelligence that I think it unlikely that mankind will ever trace out the knowledge of the universe during his tenure on earth. And yet this astonishing Individual is so motivated by love that He offered Himself in sacrifice, pain and death for us.

What are we to do with this? Should our brief lives with this, our astounding God, be primarily defined by Sundays sitting in chairs listening to brilliant messages presented by admittedly dedicated, studious men and women? No. May God forbid it. He has so much more for us, more richness, more gratifying spiritual participation, more personal, gifted, growth-inducing involvement. Will it be easy? No. Absolutely, unequivocally, no. Following God, listening for His voice, rather than doing things by rote tradition can be complex and thorny. Humbling ourselves, denying notoriety and ministry-produced finances while purposing to stay small and unnoticed will be counter-church-cultural in the extreme. Dealing with people will always be arduous. That's why Jesus, just after He had told us to treat others the way we would want to be treated, said, "Enter by the narrow gate. For the gate is wide and the way is easy that leads to destruction, and those who enter by it are many. For the gate is narrow and the way is hard that leads to life, and those who find it are few" (Matthew 7:13-14). The way that leads to destruction is easy. That's the way, I contend, we have taken. The way is hard that leads to life. Few find it.

Please join with me in discovering that way—regardless of cost.

Jim Thomson's Connection

Contact information:

Website/Blog:
jlthomson.wordpress.com

Email:
pointsofdeparture.jim@gmail.com